TRANSITS IN PLAIN ENGLISH

by Press and Ima Roberts

TABLE OF CONTENTS

Introduction 5
Transits of Pluto 7
Transits of Neptune 17
Transits of Uranus 25
Transits of Saturn 37
Transits of Jupiter 49
Transits of Mars 61
Transits of Sun 73
Transits of Venus 83
Transits of Mercury 95
Transits of New Moon 107
Transits of Full Moon 111
Transits of North Node 113
Transits of South Node 115
Transits of Moon 117
Transit Planets to Pars Fortunae 129

We wish to dedicate this book to all students of Astrology, especially to all of our students. There are three people we wish to give special thanks to: they are Stephanie Putnam, Barbie Sprouer, and Phyllis Wagner; without their helping in reading and typing this book, it would have been a much harder job.

TRANSIT ASPECTS

The most important thing to always keep in mind is that there are no bad or good aspects. It depends entirely on how you handle the aspect in your chart in relation to yourself and your environment, or, more simply, how you REACT. A SQUARE or an OPPOSITION may be a blessing in disguise and by the same token a SEXTILE or TRINE may be very destructive.

It may be helpful to think of aspects as difficult and easy or hard and soft aspects. When things are difficult they can make the individual stronger and better capable of handling his own life. When life is always easy a person may become weak and unable to handle the challenges of life when they do arise. Too much of a good thing can become bad or destructive.

MAJOR ASPECTS

EASY: CONJUNCTION   DIFFICULT: CONJUNCTION
(depending on the planets)   (depending on the planets)
TRINE   OPPOSITION
SEXTILE   SQUARE

ASPECTS IN RELATION TO TRANSITS AND PROGRESSIONS

The chart is like an alarm clock. The face of the clock is like your natal chart; showing everything that will happen to you in your life time. An aspect in the NATAL chart is like the alarm being set for a certain time. Think of a PROGRESSION as the hour hand and the TRANSIT as the minute hand. The hour hand (PROGRESSION) sets up the alarm (ASPECT), but the alarm doesn't activate until the minute hand (TRANSITING PLANET) triggers it off by contacting the aspect. All three things are necessary to make the aspect work. The progression must relate to the natal aspect and be triggered by a transiting planet.

KEY WORDS for the transiting aspect "it triggers" or "activates".

KEY WORD for the PROGRESSED aspects "PROMISES".

KEY WORDS for the NATAL aspects "It gives or denies, the promises".

Your NATAL aspects indicate what will happen over the entire life span, but it does not say when or how often. I don't believe that all natal aspects are constantly in effect. They have to be activated one way or another. This is why progressed charts or progressed aspects are important. PROGRESSED aspects are not active by themselves. They have to have something to trigger or activate them. The TRANSITING planet does this very thing.

A TRANSIT aspect does not have to be connected or aspected with the progressed chart to be active (It may not be aspected or connected in any way to the PROGRESSED CHART), but may trigger any aspect in the NATAL CHART directly without involving progressed planets.

DEGREES OF ASPECTS-PROGRESSED PLANETS

Allow one (1) degree orb approaching an aspect and one (1) leaving. THIS RULE APPLYS TO THE PROGRESSED PLANETS AND ANY PLANET IN THE NATAL CHART.

TRANSIT ASPECTS

Allow the transiting planets SUN, MOON, MERCURY AND VENUS an orb of three degrees approaching and thirty (30) minutes leaving. Allow the heavies, PLUTO, NEPTUNE, URANUS, SATURN, JUPITER AND MARS six (6) degrees approaching and one degree leaving.

TRANSIT PLUTO

KEYWORDS FOR PLUTO

POSITIVE	NEGATIVE
MONEY (LARGE AMOUNTS)	BRINGS UPHEAVALS, DISSATIS-FACTIONS, ECONOMIC WOES, FINANCIAL LOSSES
RENEWS, CHANGES AND TRANSFORMS	ILL HEALTH
RESEARCHERS	ARTHRITIS, CRIPPLED PEOPLE
INTELLECTUAL AWARENESS	BLOOD DISORDERS
CO-OPERATIVE MOVEMENTS	BURGLARS – LOSSES BY THEFT
PUBLIC FUNDS INSURANCES	COMTEMPTUOUS
SUBCONSCIOUS MIND	REBELLIOUS AND DEFIANT, LAWLESSNESS
PLACES GROUP BEFORE YOURSELF	DESTRUCTIVENESS
PROBING IN DEPTH	DISHONOR
UNIVERSAL LOVE	DRUNKENNESS
EXTREMELY LUCKY	MISTAKES
PLACES UNDERGROUND	FIRES
SEWERS	DOMINEERING AND FORCEFUL
PLUMBERS	GUILT
TECHNICIANS	IMMODEST
SURGEONS	INSANITY
MORTICIANS	
DETECTIVES	OVER PASSIONATE
PUBLIC AWARENESS	EXTREME ANGER AND TEMPER FLARE UPS
	GOSSIP AND LIARS
	EXTREME BAD LUCK

PLUTO TRANSITS IN THE HOUSES

HOUSES

1. There is an intense desire to be more independent. For women this could lead to a romance. For men this placement may cause him to want to go into business for himself. You may completely change your outlook and attitude about life.

2. You may stew and fret about children and business. You may have an intense desire to speculate. The source of your income may change and you may change your attitude about spending this income. By being overly concerned about increasing your income, you may become involved in questionable transactions.

3. You may make friends with younger people, who are more aggressive and energetic. May become bored and restless and take more short trips than usual. Your brothers and sisters or neighbors may move at this time. You may start classes in more progressive and scientific subjects.

4. You may attempt to assume a more authoritative role in your business and at home. You may move from the country to the city. The younger people may rebel against the authority of the parents. You may invest in mining or real estate property

5. Your approach to your children's education will be more liberal. may speculate or go on a gambling spree. You may be able to influence the younger people because of your more revolutionary ideas. You may take up a new hobby that may turn into a source of income.

6. Might bring back old memories, so you may be able to re-evaluate them more objectively. You may change your job for a better one. May find yourself becoming more interested in psychic subjects. May find that you possess a unique talent that can help others.

7. You may meet many new people during this time. Some will become close friends and the others will pass out of your life or they may become business partners. You may lose some older friends because of some disagreements. May be divorced and re-married during this period. Carelessness may cause unexpected law suit. Many of your open enemies will be dealt with and defeated.

8. You may be placed in the position of authority over a large group of people. Credit will be so easy to get that you may have a tendency to over borrow. May make permanent changes in your will. Some may enter medical school or research. The wife may return to her profession or work.

9. Take care that this position doesn't give you too much energy and confidence, which may be offensive to those around you. Tension and restlessness may cause students to drop out of college or become involved in riots and mob gatherings. Some of you will move to foreign countries. This position may cause you to completely change your religion or church. It may appear that your in-laws are moving every time you hear from them. There may be an intense desire to educate yourself.

10.   Your desire for success and increase in income may be much greater. Some may consider returning to their old profession or jobs. Others may completely change their professions or jobs. There may be an intense desire for fame and success. There may be a complete change in domestic relationships; the wife may become the chief breadwinner.

11.   You may become very involved with affairs of relatives. Your friends will probably be younger and more energetic. Progressive clubs and associations may interest you more at this time. Some casual friends may assist you in obtaining something long hoped for or desired.

12.   This is a period of intense internal readjustment. You may find yourself getting rid of old and useless ideas. Some may become involved in transforming a school, institution or building into something new. Many become involved in prison reforms. This is a very good time to re-evaluate health problems.

TRANSITS ASPECTS OF THE PLANETS TO NATAL PLANETS

PLUTO TO SUN

CONJUNCT — This aspect will increase your desire for independence. You may be more agressive about your aims and goals. There may be important changes in your life that will point you in an entirely different direction. There may be much tension going on within you at this time, which will make you become very restless. Some women will change marriage partners. If you have any chronic complaints, this aspect may aggravate it. This is a good time to have a complete physical check-up.

SEXTILE — Your personal interest will turn towards your friends and their pleasures. You probably have many opportunities to join some sort of organizations and to participate in activities within these same organizations at this time. You may become very interested now in some sort of research project.

SQUARE — Your plans and desires may be interfered with by a relative or friend. Don't be demanding or too aggressive at this time because it may cause you many emotional upsets.

TRINE — A partner or friend may give you some valuable advice that maybe you should heed. You could form some sort of partnership with some one you like and respect very much.

OPPOSITION — May become very interested in forming some sort of partnership with some one. The new people you come in contact with are more aggressive and may try to lead you into some sort of new venture that may not turn out so well. You and old partner may be separated at this time. Think twice about every decision that you make but do act.

PLUTO TO MOON

CONJUNCT — Your emotions may be easily aroused at this time; don't push things and become too impulsive. Pay more attention to other's opinions.

SEXTILE — You will have a more positive attitude. There will be more pleasant contacts made in your social circles.

SQUARE — You may want changes at this time just for the sake of changes. There may not be any valid reasons for the desire for these changes. Don't push your opinions on others. Relax and let things happen as they will.

TRINE — This is a good time to reconsider old problems and for finding more positive solutions for them. May at this time change your entire approach to life with positive results.

OPPOSITION — There may be a change in partnerships now. You may try a new approach and will be influenced by a new male friend.

PLUTO TO MERCURY

CONJUNCT
Your mind may be concerned about children, speculation or business. You may have new ideas about how to express yourself. Some may have much tension and nervousness, caused by this aspect, and may become very restless. Some one may gossip about you.

SEXTILE
Most of your thinking will be about your romances. This aspect may increase your popularity. This could be a very favorable time for associating with children and to become very concerned about their education.

SQUARE
There may be a separation with a relative over an argument about religious beliefs. May have quarrels and arguments with borthers and sisters. Troubles with the in-laws, who may bring a lawsuit against you. Don't drive too fast because you may receive a speeding ticket.

TRINE
This stimulates your mind and your thinking. You may become very interested at this time in telepathy or hypnosis.

OPPOSITION
Being too outspoken and quarrelsome may cause you problems with the people around you. Be careful that you don't write something now that could cause you trouble later. May have an intense desire to do some traveling due to your restlessness. You may become intently aware of your lack of education. Salesmen, writers and teachers may experience doubt as to whether they are in the right profession. They could be thinking about changing their profession.

PLUTO TO VENUS

CONJUNCT
You may find that your social life has been very active. You may make more friends that are aggressive and active.

SEXTILE
You will find at this time that your social life is more active and you are more popular. May become more interested in younger people and thier viewpoints. May find a slight increase in your finances.

SQUARE
Some relative may give you a bad time about your love affairs or romances. May be some legal difficulties caused by your in-laws. Be careful about your driving habits at this time or you may get in trouble with the law.

TRINE
May find that you enjoy social affairs much more. You are more popular and may have more than one love affair going on. This is a time that you will enjoy the company of children more.

OPPOSITION
The new people you meet now are more exciting and enjoyable. May have a romance with a younger person. There may be a change in your marriage or your love life.

PLUTO TO JUPITER

CONJUNCT
May be tempted to resist authority or those in authority. May mean a tremendous increase in your finances. A lucky period.

SEXTILE
A very good time to change jobs and to make a change in the home. This is a very good time to start any new projects.

SQUARE
The plans of relatives or friends may conflict with yours. Don't force your opinions on the boss or those that are close to you.

TRINE
You should find yourself getting along with others better. Don't overexert yourself now. Make sure that you get plenty of rest and sleep.

OPPOSITION
You may be threatened with a law suit or there may be people that are gossiping about you for no apparant reason. Be very careful of your health. You may be over optimistic at this time and an impulsive decision may cause you a loss in your income or finances. Be very careful about your reputation at this time.

PLUTO TO MARS

CONJUNCT
This aspect may cause you to become to aggressive. Watch your temper at this time because the least little thing may irritate you. All of this excess energy may offend others so take it easy.

SEXTILE
Much can be accomplished in secret or seclusion. Don't try to push yourself before the public. This is a good time to overcome any psychological problems you may have. By helping others, you will be helping yourself.

SQUARE
You may become too impulsive and this could cause you to be argumentative or quarrelsome. Slow down and don't drive too fast because you may have an accident. Your temper is bombastic at this time. Keep it under control. Too much tension and stress may cause health problems.

TRINE
Your creative talents are very prominent at this time. You may be so energetic that it is impossible for you to be still. Take up a physical fitness program to help you control this excessive amount of energy. You may want to speculate or gamble.

OPPOSITION
You may be very irritating and quarrelsome. Accidents could be caused by carelessness. If all of this energy is kept under control, this time could give very constructive results.

PLUTO TO SATURN

CONJUNCT This could be a very favorable time for you to go into business for yourself. May have a favorable romance now. Be energetic and progressive in everything you do.

SEXTILE Your energetic and enthusiastic approach to your work will impress those in authority or your boss. You may have an intense desire to speculate or gamble. You may receive an increase in your income.

SQUARE You probably will seek a greater authority over your own affairs. You may resent any attempt by anyone to tell you what to do. You could be more creative at this time.

TRINE You will be full of vim and vigor. You will do things you didn't think possible. This is a good time to build a foundation for some future project. You will find yourself more self-sufficient and more independent.

OPPOSITION You may get the idea that everything is going against you but this is not so. What you may be trying to do at this date will manifest itself at a later date. You may be tempted to rebel against all forms of authority.

PLUTO TO URANUS

CONJUNCT NEVER HAPPENS IN A LIFE TIME

SEXTILE You may have some very unusual ideas and opinions now. Check them to see if they are reliable before you try them out. You may become interested in studying some occult subject.

SQUARE This may be a very competitive time. You may be bucking authority because you are trying to gain control of yourself. This could cause separation with those you are resisting. This could cause physical violence to be used against you or you may be tempted to use physical force yourself. Your attitude at this time might be "Might makes right".

TRINE You may become very creative and original in whatever you do. May become very interested in bringing about changes. These changes can be made without any stress or trouble to you.

OPPOSITION You may have trouble getting along with others. This could bring about sudden unexpected and abrupt changes in your life. Opportunities may come in unexpected ways or manner. This also could bring about a change that has been long waited for.

PLUTO TO NEPTUNE

CONJUNCT You could be very practical now or you could be carried away with your daydreaming. Use caution in settling estates or anything that has to do with tax matters.

SEXTILE   You may find that you are becoming more interested in religious and philosophical matters instead of being interested in physical and material gains.

SQUARE   You may find that you will have to face up to the vague ideas or false concepts from the past. Don't daydream so much. Explain all of your ideas and plans very thoroughly to prevent misunderstandings.

TRINE   This may be a very good time to change your will or change your plans for the future. Take care of all tax matters.

OPPOSITION   NEVER HAPPENS IN A LIFE TIME

PLUTO TO PLUTO

CONJUNCT NEVER HAPPENS IN A LIFE TIME.

SEXTILE   You may go into a partnership with someone to gain financially. May get involved in a research project with someone else.

SQUARE   You may spend too much money on a friend or the advice of a friend may cause you to lose money. This is a bad time for borrowing or loaning money from a friend. Some organization could cause you trouble regarding your savings or insurance policy. Taxes could be a headache now.

TRINE   You will have plenty of opportunities to get rid of the useless things or people in your life. This is an excellent time to try new methods to improve your health.

OPPOSITION: NEVER HAPPENS IN A LIFE TIME.

TRANSIT NEPTUNE

KEYWORDS FOR NEPTUNE

POSITIVE

IDEALISTIC; FAITH
ARTISTS AND MUSICIANS

WISDOM
OCCULTISM
OVER REACTS
READILY CONFORMS TO
GROUP
AIR TRAVEL
ALCOHOLIC BEVERAGES
BALLET
BARTENDERS
BEACHES
BOATS
BORROWING
CORPORATE BUSINESSES
CHARITY

CHURCHES
DENTURES
DETECTIVES
GLASSES
HOSPITAL WORKERS

NEGATIVE

DAYDREAMING
DECEIVES, HIDES
HYPOCRISIES
ALLURES, ENTICES
NERVOUSNESS
APPREHENSION
VAGUE FEARS

EMBARRASSING
LACKS SELF CONFIDENCE
BETRAYALS
BLUFFING
CONFIDENCE MEN
CONFINEMENTS
DRUNKENNESS
EMOTIONAL DEPRESSIONS
FEELINGS ARE HURT
EASILY
PROBLEMS WITH FEET
INFERIORITY COMPLEXES
DEFRAUDS
TEMPTATIONS

TRANSIT NEPTUNE IN THE HOUSES

HOUSES

1. Life is more glamorous and exciting now. Guard your reputation and also guard against any possibility of a scandal. Be very practical and keep your emotions under control. There may be plenty of opportunities to obtain new friends but be very selective or they may deceive you.

2. Money comes to you in unexpected ways. At the same time, it may disappear because of unforseen expenses. You are more sympathetic towards others.

3. Your contact with your brothers and sisters will be more enjoyable. Also, your social contact with your relatives will be rewarding. People at this time may reveal their inner most secrets to you. Your thoughts and ideas will be very inspirational.

4. Gossip or some type of scandal may disturb you very much at this time. Watch your consumption of all alcoholic beverages and drugs because there may be ill affects to your health.

5. You may become very interested in investing in a motion picture, or oil and shipping. Your creative ideas now are very inspirational and constructive. You may find that you will develop a new business, in addition to what you are doing now.

6. Your co-workers, associates or employees may give you some sort of assistance at this time. Guard your health against all excessess. Be extra careful of drugs and alcohol.

7. This position may bring you in contact with people who have some sort of mental problem. You may go to work in some institution or a hospital. Take care that you are not deceived by a partner or close friend.

8. If you are handling other people's money, be extra careful you are not tempted to use it for your own personal use. You may receive some money from an insurance policy or legacy, but there will be a lot of confusion involved before it will be settled satisfactorily. Watch your health at this time.

9. May take a trip by water to a foreign country. You may become interested in investigating some form of psychic phenomenon. You may have trouble organizing your knowledge or thoughts because this may be a difficult time for you to concentrate.

10. One of your superiors or those in authority above you in your profession may be involved in a scandal and try to involve you. The promotion the boss promised may not materialize.

11. Your social life will be more active. You may meet someone of the opposite sex at a social function that will fascinate you. This could bring about a closer relationship with your relatives.

12. This position may cause a lot of mental confusion. You may become more careless with your finances. Don't let your emotions cause you to lose contact with reality.

TRANSIT NEPTUNE ASPECTS

NEPTUNE TO MOON

CONJUNCT · You may run into many deceptive people in public and business relationships. Be very cautious. Check everything twice. Make sure all of your dealings with people are above-board. Stay away from controversy of any kind. Do not argue with anyone at this time.

SEXTILE You may find a solution to an old problem, but you may have problems in trying to explain the solution to anyone else.

SQUARE Your thinking is very confused at this time. Any emotional upset now will interfere with your reasoning. May have arguments with mother or wife at this time.

TRINE Your emotions and thinking are more under control during this period. You may have an intense desire to help those around you. This is a good time to attend public functions or to give a party yourself.

OPPOSITION You may have some inspirational ideas and thoughts, but your timing seems to be way off. Listen to all the facts before you make any decisions because you may jump to conclusions.

NEPTUNE TO MERCURY

CONJUNCT You may have some very inspirational thoughts and ideas at this time, but your thoughts tend to be disjointed and dis-organized. Your intuition is very strong at this time. Any facts you may receive at this time may be confused or deceptive. Wait until a later time to make any important decisions. Read all the fine print in any contract you may sign at this time.

SEXTILE Your interest may have a strong leaning towards magnetic healing, occultism and related fields.

SQUARE Your thinking may be very confused and will have trouble concentrating for any length of time. You may try to learn too many things at this point. Don't gossip or listen to any. Facts tend to be stretched now.

TRINE This is a productive time for writers because this aspect helps increase the imagination and the intuition. You may read some very inspirational books now.

OPPOSITION This aspect may bring you into contact with fiction writers and poets. You may have trouble concentrating. You may feel slightly suspicious of all people and any events. You may take everything that is said or done around you as if it was entirely directed at you.

NEPTUNE TO VENUS

CONJUNCT
Your intense romantic feeling could possibly deceive you at this time. You may have a tendency to look at the world through rose colored glasses. You may intentionally deceive the one who you're having a love affair with or they will deceive you.

SEXTILE
This is a very creative time in your life and you will probably be more inclined to be poetic than usual. This aspect may make your social life more active and make you more interested in your love affairs. This could increase financial program or bring you a promotion at work.

SQUARE
This could possibly make your social life more exciting. This could bring a very important love affair into your life, but, at the same time, the lover could be deceiving you.

TRINE
If you're interested in the dramatic arts, this could be a very good time for you. You are more diplomatic and pleasant in your social contacts and with friends.

OPPOSITION
You may become involved with some people who are involved in sort of a scandal. Your social life will be more active and exciting. Could become aware that your true love is deceiving you in some way or another.

NEPTUNE TO SUN

CONJUNCT
The people that you may get involved with may be very unrealistic or too aggressive. You may be thinking seriously of searching for the ideal love affair or lover. You may at this time be investigating a possibility of entering some sort of Utopian community or become involved in some sort of Utopian Project.

SEXTILE
You may become very interested in joining some philosophical order or church. You are very interested at this time in studying religious and philosophical books.

SQUARE
Your judgement may be faulty at this time and others may influence your decisions too much. You may be daydreaming too much, when you should be more actively striving for your goals.

TRINE
There may be many spontaneous psychic and spiritual experiences now. You will feel more in harmony with your friends and relatives.

OPPOSITION
Your judgement may be faulty, causing you to be deceived by those you come in contact with. There may be many mistakes made by you at this time. Make sure that you are punctual and prompt for all appointments you may have. Rest and relax more because you may be very nervous and tense.

NEPTUNE TO MARS

CONJUNCT
You may become to fanatical about your religious belief or your philosophy. Be very careful that you don't become too engrossed in obtaining material things or in some type of sensual enjoyment. You may be very lucky in love and business.

SEXTILE
You can accomplish very much at this time if you are practical in everything you do. Don't be carried away with your daydreaming.

SQUARE
You may become so involved in doing others a favor that you may have little time for your own projects. You may ask advice from husband or father and then argue with them about the advice. Use the utmost caution while dealing with the opposite sex.

TRINE
You may become interested in studying some occult subject at this time, to develop your own psychic abilities. You may be feeling extra glamorous and attractive now.

OPPOSITION
You may be attracted to some sort of sensational thing that may cause you some trouble with others. You may realize that at this time some middle age man (or woman) has been deceiving you.

NEPTUNE TO JUPITER

CONJUNCT
May become very interested in studying religious or philosophical subjects. You may find that your intuition is more accurate now.

SEXTILE
May become very interested in taking some long distance trip or dreaming about the possibility. You may enjoy attending some sort of church service regularly. There may be unexpected financial gain.

SQUARE
You could be deceived because of your judgement being impaired at this time in that you don't get all the facts about people or circumstances. May make promises that you could not possibly keep.

TRINE
This aspect could put you in contact with some very important people. Your philosophical attitude is very positive about life in general. Some may become interested in joining a church or religious order.

OPPOSITION
You may come in contact with some very unusual psychic people and may have some unusual psychic experience yourself. Don't gamble or speculate because your judgement may be poor.

NEPTUNE TO SATURN

CONJUNCT This is a confusing aspect. You could be blamed for others mistakes. You could come in contact with some very positive people that would help you to develop your creative talents.

SEXTILE Those in authority will be more receptive to your inspirational and creative ideas. Many opportunities may come your way from large corporations or big businesses.

SQUARE Those in authority may criticize you because of your radical ideas against the establishment. Stay away from any type of speculation. You should become aware that your dreams will not be fulfilled without a lot of hard work. You may have a lot of vague and unfounded fears at this time.

TRINE This is the time to really develop your creative ideas and talents. Don't be so impulsive in your judgement. Be super practical in everything you do.

OPPOSITION You may find at this time that you will run into competition from some elderly person. You may have trouble or be deceived in some real estate transaction. You may come in contact with people with mental problems.

NEPTUNE TO URANUS

CONJUNCT May have dreams of doing great things and may try to accomplish them. You may succeed in some of these things but not all of them.

SEXTILE Those in authority will give you credit for your positive attitude and the hard work you have done. Don't let this go to your head. Your pride may become a problem at this time.

SQUARE This aspect can cause a lot of nervousness and confusion. You should relax more in this period. This may cause you to move your home from one place to another. Make sure you finish anything started at this time.

TRINE You may want to speculate or gamble on about everything. You may have many psychic experiences at this time but you will probably deny them. This could help you in finding unusual type of job.

OPPOSITION There may be a lot of deception going on around you at work or in your social life. Check the validity of all information that you receive at this time. You may deceive yourself because of your confused thinking or be so self-confident that you will believe that you could not fail at anything but you probably will.

NEPTUNE TO NEPTUNE

CONJUNCT   DOESN'T HAPPEN IN A LIFE TIME

SEXTILE   The people that you think would never deceive you will and will cause a lot of emotional upset. No matter how much people deceive you at this time, make sure that you are honest and above-board.

SQUARE   No matter what you may try to do or say at this time, people will be suspicious of you. Be extra careful of your reputation. You could be doing too much daydreaming during this period.

TRINE   Your intuition is very reliable at this time. You may begin to realize that what you have been stewing and worrying about really is trivial. You may have a clearer insight into your life at this time.

OPPOSITION   VERY SELDOM HAPPENS

NEPTUNE TO PLUTO

CONJUNCT   CANNOT HAPPEN IN A LIFE TIME

SEXTILE   This is a good time to try out your new and creative ideas. There may be an intense desire to break from old routines.

SQUARE   Don't be too aggressive or pushy now. If you start anything at this time, make sure you complete it before you start something else. You may become involved in sensational things, which will cause you dis-illusionment. Get all facts before starting anything.

TRINE   Your intuition may become more accurate and greatly increased at this time. You may become more independent without any big problems. You'll be more creative and will be able to develop your creative talents with less effort.

OPPOSITION   Be extra careful around water. Undue restlessness may cause you to be very careless. You may become very rebellious towards anything that may have to do with the establishment or anything traditional. Any new plans instituted now should be very practical.

TRANSIT URANUS

KEYWORDS FOR URANUS

POSITIVE	NEGATIVE
BRINGS UNEXPECTED OPPORTUNITIES AND SURPRISES	BREAKS UP MARRIAGES, ROMANCES AND FRIENDSHIPS
CRAFTSMEN, ENGINEERS ASTROLOGERS, MECHANICS AND ELECTRICIANS	SEPARATIONS OF ALL KINDS
UNEXPECTED VISIT FROM PEOPLE FROM FAR OFF	COMPULSIVE BEHAVIOR
UNEXPECTED CRISES IN LIFE OR EXTREME CHANGES IN LIFE, NEW AND BETTER WAYS OF LIFE	MOODINESS AND TOUCHINESS
GOOD TRAVELING	UNEXPECTED ILLNESS
RAILROAD PEOPLE	MEETINGS OF ODD AND ECCENTRIC PEOPLE IN NEGATIVE WAYS
CHAUFFEURS	MUCH TENSION AND NERVOUSNESS
VERY ACTIVE, INDEPENDENT AND ENTERPRISING	ANGER, IRRITABILITY
ATTRACTIVE TO OPPOSITE SEX	IMPULSIVE AND RASH SPEECH
ACTIVATES THE THINKING	DISORGANIZED
YOUR JUDGEMENT IS GOOD	ACCIDENTS
FREEDOM	VERY ABRUPT AND TACTLESS
INTUITIVE	UNCONVENTIONAL LOVE AFFAIRS AFFAIRS
ORGANIZED	ALIMONY
THOSE IN AUTHORITY	BANKRUPTCY
BACHELORS	BIZARRE THINGS
CARS	BOSSY PEOPLE
CLUBS	DEMANDING
COMPETITORS	DIVORCES
DRIVERS OF AUTOMOBILES	
FREE WILL	

URANUS TRANSITS IN THE HOUSES

HOUSES

1. You may be so restless at this time that you'll desire any changes just for the sake of change. You may become very bored with all routine things. You will become extremely independent at this time. This placement could cause you to take impulsive trips. This could also cause many people to impulsively get married. There may be some very radical changes in your speech and mode of dress. You will become attracted to many unusual or scientific people.

2. There may be many unusual and unexpected opportunities for you to improve your earning power. This unexpected gain may be spent just as fast as it is received. You may be tempted to borrow money that is not necessary, or become interested in "get rich" schemes that have no possibility of succeeding. Your income is very unreliable.

3. You may take many impulsive short trips that may cause you trouble. You will probably meet very unusual people while on these trips. You may buy a car unexpectedly or receive some sort of communication from brothers and sisters that will contain unusual or shocking news. You may become interested in studying astrology, occult or metaphysical subjects. You may receive information about plans or ideas that could be favorable or adverse. Your mind may be so active that you will have trouble concentrating on any single thing at this time.

4. May bring about many drastic changes in domestic affairs. You may move from one town to another. The younger people may move out of the parent's home to establish one of their own. You may move out of a house into an apartment. You may unexpectedly invest in an unusual piece of real estate. Circumstance may force an unexpected separation from one of the parents.

5. You may become involved in an unconventional love affair that could cause you problems. You may become interested in many "get rich" schemes, or speculation or gambling of some sort. You may meet important people who can help you with your creative ideas or schemes. You may take up an unusual hobby or unplanned children may be born at this time. May take many trips because of your intense desire for fun and recreation; these trips may be caused by an excessive amount of tension within you.

6. You may have an unexpected opportunity to acquire a new job in an entirely different field than you have ever worked before. This could bring you an unexpected promotion because of your creative and unusual ideas. Also, at the same time, you could possibly be laid off from a job without any warning. Your health may suffer because of nervousness and tension. You may have unexpected dental problems at this time if there is any adverse aspect. You may become involved in some unusual type of health treatment, such as acupuncture treatment. You may find that you can borrow money or obtain credit without any great effort.

7.	This position could bring an unusual number of competitive people into your life. Older people could unexpectedly sell their business and retire. This planet could bring on unusual neuritis, nervous complaints, or could cause an operation. There may be unexpected marriages or separation between partners. There may be unusual differences in ages in marriages at this time. You could be asked to make some impromptu speeches in public. There may be many kinds of contracts come up at this time for consideration. You could become involved in unexpected lawsuits.

8.	You may receive an unexpected legacy but may have trouble collecting it. Your partner's financial rpogram may be very unreliable at this time. You may become interested in taking out a life insurance policy or in writing out your will. May have an unusual sexual experience or your sexual desire may be very intense at this time. You may begin some sort of research project. You may become interested in studying Astrology, or some other occult subject. You may have trouble with income taxes or receive some unexpected refund from your income tax. You may be asked to manage other people's money at this time.

9.	Your thoughts may turn toward obtaining some sort of higher education. You may become interested in studying some philosophical or religious subject. You may desire to take a long distance trip to broaden your knowledge of the world. You may become involved in divorce proceedings or some sort of a lawsuit. Your mind may be so active that you could have trouble concentrating on any one thing for any length of time. This would be a very good time for writers and authors to deal with their publishers. This is a favorable time to deal with large corporations or government officials.

10.	This could bring about unexpected honors and success. This also could bring about more power or authority in your profession. You could unexpectedly go into an entirely different profession. You could move your home because of a transfer in work. You may find areas in your social life unexpectedly rewarding. You could become a professional astrologer at this time.

11.	You may become very interested in joining some group, society or brotherhood. You may receive help from groups, societies or friends to obtain some goals you have been working for. You may be making new friends and at the same time losing old ones. You may be having trouble with step-children. You may unexpectedly be promoted or gain recognition in your profession.

12.	You may find that you will be able to get rid of some old responsibility or old troubles. You may receive undeserved rewards at this time. You may be confined to some institution. May have to reorganize your financial program because of reduced income due to illness. You may become involved in some type of research project, This is not the time to do anything in an impulsive way or to become too independent. This is a good time to ask advice from older or reliable people.

TRANSIT URANUS ASPECTS

URANUS TO MOON

CONJUNCT
Many emotional changes is the KEY WORD. Very intense tension and nervousness could cause health problems. Bachelors may become involved with married women. This could be a very creative time. This aspect could cause trouble with mother, wife or women. Many upheavels in your domestic affairs. You may revamp your style of dress or your speech.

SEXTILE
This is a good time to start any new project in which the public will participate. Watch for any opportunity to improve your business. Don't hesitate to take the expert's advice or any reliable friend's advice.

SQUARE
Your mind seems to be working at lightening speed. You can accomplish things in a third of the time it usually takes you. This is the trouble, you have a tendency at this time to overlook the little things. Slow down. The least little thing could throw you into a temper tantrum. Relax and keep your temper under control. This tension could cause you to be careless and cause an accident in traffic. Drive slower or you will have trouble with the law.

TRINE
You may think of unusual ideas on how to remodel your home, or to help with domestic affairs. This is a good time to impress the public with your creative ideas. You could become very magnetic to the opposite sex.

OPPOSITION
This aspect could cause you to separate from your wife, mother or an older sister. You may move from your house to an apartment in town. You may want to invest in an unusual piece of real estate.

URANUS TO MERCURY

CONJUNCT
This is a good time to study astrology or any occult subject. You may become very nervous and temperamental at this time. Many opportunities may appear that would be beneficial for you. You may take many unexpected trips. You may be able to speak at some public function. May become very intuitive at this time.

SEXTILE
This is a good time for you to get caught up on all correspondence. You will be very fluent now in expressing yourself and would be a good time to study because your concentration is good. You may receive a compliment or recognition from something you had done in the past.

SQUARE	This aspect could make you extremely nervous and tense. You may have an intense desire to write, but your radical views may get you into trouble with those in positions of power. You could be very argumentative and will have a strong desire to push things through. If you would take it easier, things would be done in a more positive way. This could cause disagreement with younger people. This could also cause an accident because you're in such a hurry to get some place. You could make wrong decisions at this time because of your impulsiveness.
TRINE	This would be a very good time for you to present your unusual and creative ideas to the public. This also would be a good time to take a short trip to see friends and relatives. May come in contact with unusual people who will become close friends.
OPPOSITION	You may have a tendency to become very irritable with anyone that doesn't agree with you. You may be so tense and nervous that you could have trouble sleeping. Your thinking and your memory may be very poor at this time because you're so tense and nervous. Avoid being sarcastic or argumentative with those around you. Be very cautious about your driving.

URANUS TO VENUS

CONJUNCT	A very active and lively social life. This aspect could bring new love affairs and friendships. Your emotions and affections are very unreliable at this time. You may come in contact with very unconventional and unusual people at this time. Could bring very good results in regards to your profession and business. You will be able to express your creative ideas or develop your artistic talents.
SEXTILE	You may have an unusual romantic affair at this time. Good time to buy clothing or jewelry. This would be a good time for a trip to the beauty shop. You may get rid of old clothes and start wearing the new styles.
SQUARE	An unexpected argument may cause you to separate from a lover or sweetheart. You may form an unconventional relationship with the opposite sex. The affair may only be for a short period and then you will part company. This aspect may cause many embarrassing scenes at a social affair. May loose money unexpectedly through your own carelessness. You may make many new friends but separate from old friends.
TRINE	This could cause you to become very popular and receive many invitations to parties. This aspect usually brings luck and gifts into your life. Any new love affair started now usually lasts. You may become interested in studying music or painting.
OPPOSITION	This aspect has a peculiar affect on the emotions. You may become involved with an individual whose life style is entirely different than yours. You may become very angry or jealous at this time. Your feelings may be easily hurt.

URANUS TO SUN

CONJUNCT

You could become very restless and nervous at this time. You may become very ambitious and this could cause you to seek out people in the place of authority. There may be many big changes occurring in your life. You may have many opportunities now and they will seem to fall from the clouds. You may suffer from some type of anxiety because things are not moving fast enough to suit you.

SEXTILE

This is a favorable time to ask favors of those in the position of authority. There will be nothing consistent about this aspect, but it will bring positive results if a person makes an effort.

SQUARE

This aspect will probably make you very nervous and tense. This could also cause accidents because of carelessness on your part. You may become very aggressive and argumentative at this time. This could cause a separation or divorce. This is a bad aspect to get married under. You could have nervous diseases and different complaints of obscure types. You could also have many muscle spasms. You could antagonize those in authority and get in trouble for this. This could cause unexpected separation with males in business or in the domestic life. You could be very busy but not accomplish much. Your energy is probably wasted with just moving around.

TRINE

This could make men very attractive to the opposite sex. You could become very inventive or ingenious at this time. You would be able to present your ideas to others with ease. You may become very unconventional in your sex life. A good time to begin any new creative project.

OPPOSITION

This aspect usually causes much tension and nervousness. May make you very impatient with the old ways of doing things and want to adopt new ones. You may antagonize those you work with, or your friends, or those in business because of your impatience. Many things that appear to be promising may fall through at the last moment. You could make many mistakes at this time because of your impatience and you will try to force things to happen instead of letting them happen. Group activities may attract you now.

URANUS TO MARS

CONJUNCT

You may become involved in many accidents because you're in too big of a hurry. This could be a very strong sex aspect. You may rebel so strongly against existing conditions that you could make those around you very angry with you. This could cause a divorce. You may become very impulsive and this could make you act very foolhardy or to be overconfident.

SEXTILE	This is a very favorable aspect for your profession, business or your romantic life. This will give you many inspirational ideas and give you the courage to carry them out. Your intuition is very strong now. You may have more moral and physical courage with this aspect in force.
SQUARE	This could make you foolhardy and reckless. You may have many accidents and health problems because you'll overdo everything. May become involved in many arguments because you're in a hurry and don't want to wait. You may have toubles with muscle spasms and teeth problems. Don't speculate, gamble or become involved in any dangerous sports, such as hunting, mountain climbing, or camping trips.
TRINE	You may become more daring and take more chances without adverse results. This would be a very good time to speculate or gamble. This aspect could cause you to do something daring or courageous. You may find that you can become more ingenious or inventive about machinery. Your intuition is very strong and may make its effect shown in unusual ways.
OPPOSITION	You may impulsively divorce your partner and be sorry for it at a later date. You may be over-confident in all areas of your life and make many gross mistakes because your decisions were impulsively made. You may have trouble sleeping because of tension and nervousness. This could cause many accidents because you're in too big of a hurry. Do not have any sort of operation under this aspect. Be very careful around machinery and electrical appliances.

URANUS TO JUPITER

CONJUNCT	You may become very interested in or take unexpected journeys. You may become very interested in studying some sort of higher education, such as philosophy and religion. Do not speculate or gamble or the results may be very disastrous. This aspect could bring to completion some project you have been working on for years. Don't become involved in any "get rich" schemes.
SEXTILE	There may be many opportunities for help in your profession. Make sure that you don't make any decisions without careful consideration.
SQUARE	Don't speculate or gamble at this time because there's a possibility of financial losses. You may loose a position of authority or a job. Don't push things at this time because your judgement and timing may be off. This is a treacherous aspect for the finances. Make plans and wait until a later time to carry them out.
TRINE	This is a very lucky period. You may become very interested in or actually make a long distance trip. You may become interested in some progressive method of learning. This is a good time to study Astrology, philosophy or religion. This is a good time to present your publisher with your book. This is a lucky aspect. You are more understanding and sympathetic.

OPPOSITION   You may find yourself getting rid of old and out moded ideas about education, philosophy and religion. Authority appears to be opposing you because of their lack of understanding of what you're trying to do. This may bring you in contact with people involved in publishing, travel, education, astrology or religion. You may find yourself dealing with lawyers and judges more than usual. Your inlaws may cause you trouble with this aspect in force.

URANUS TO SATURN

CONJUNCT   This aspect could make you think that your entire life is being shattered. You find that you have to learn new ways and methods in life, which is very disturbing. You appear to be pulled two different ways at once. In the end you may find that your temper has become very vicious. Your marriage or partnerships may be very frustrating and troublesome. You may have many problems with elderly males or elderly people.

SEXTILE   Your new and progressive ideas will be accepted more at this time from those in authority. This aspect will cause you to become more determined to see projects finished. This is a good time to start any project that needs time to complete. This is a very good aspect for doing long range planning.

SQUARE   This is what is called the accident aspect. There's a tendency here for broken bones. Don't start any dental work, wait. A very frustrating time because of many delays and disappointments. The temper is very vicious now because of above things. Learn to sit and wait until this aspect is over, which will be quite some time. Elderly people in the position of authority may appear to be against you. May have many quarrels with father or some older male.

TRINE   This is a good time to seriously study because your concentration is very good. Many unexpected things in life will be very positive. This is a very good aspect to start any long range project that will take years to complete.

OPPOSITION   You may begin to feel that some heavy responsibility has been lifted from your shoulders. There may be a lot of internal emotional conflicts because the old has to be gotten rid of and you will have to learn to handle new ideas and find new methods of handling your problems. You may find that you are opposing those in authority or they are opposing you.

URANUS TO URANUS

CONJUNCT   There could be unexpected loss of old friends or you could become very interested in making new friends; who are more pioneering or more progressive and active in their attitudes or aims. You may feel that you have an unexpected surge of energy or physical strength. Life seems to become more interesting at this time and this will probably cause you to take some unusual studies of some sort; like becoming interested in studying Astrology or some related metaphysical subject. This could be a very tense time for you. This aspect usually happens around the age of 84 to 85 years of age.

SEXTILE   You will have the opportunity to institute any progressive changes in your life that you feel necessary. As the result of these changes you bring about, you will be given an opportunity to receive help from others.

SQUARE   This comes about the age of twenty-one (21), when one usually starts to declare his or her independence. This could be a very critical time in your life. Don't let your emotions cause you to become too radical just to show your independence, or it will cause you to be separated from your loved ones. Take it easy and relax as much as possible.

TRINE   You may become very intuitive at this time and you may find that you can depend on your intuitions. The odd things in your life that are not very productive will begin to drop from your life; this could include old friends and associates. This will be a very progressive time in your life.

OPPOSITION This aspect could indicate an important change in your life. You will be attracted to new and progressive people and they will be attracted to you. There is much tension and nervousness under this aspect which could put a lot of stress on the physical body. If proper health care has been observed, this may not bother you but if not, you may have some serious health problem. You may completely change your entire philosophical or religious goals in your life. The more flexible you are the easier this period will be for you. This aspect could bring about achievements you have been working toward for many years. It all depends on how well a person has prepared for this time of his life.

URANUS TO NEPTUNE

CONJUNCT   There may be many spontaneous psychic events in your life that may be very frightening. You may have many prophetic dreams. This could cause much confusion in your life. Most of the results from this aspect depend on the aspects to your natal Neptune. This could cause you to rebel against all phony and hypercritical religious practices. This is an agnostic aspect and has a tendency to upset all traditional beliefs and practices.

SEXTILE	Your friends or a member of your club may help you to gain in some way. You may receive assistance from various clubs or societies.
SQUARE	Many deceptive and negative influences may be felt in business and social life. You may have various promoters trying to get you to invest in many "get rich" schemes. Don't get involved in public life or you'll be very disappointed. Don't let your imagination run away with itself. Accept advice from a reliable friend or expert because your judgement is faulty at this time.
TRINE	Your ingenuity or inspirational ideas are very good at this time, especially with any thing to do with electricity or astrology or occult matters. May make new friends that will turn out to be very reliable. You may become very interested in studying astrology or some other occult subject.
OPPOSITION	NEVER HAPPENS IN A LIFE TIME.

URANUS TO PLUTO

CONJUNCT	You may become more interested in young people and their creativeness and may become more personally involved with them. You may become very involved in some research project.
SEXTILE	Someone may give an unexpected financial support for some research project you're involved in. This aspect will give you the determination and courage to carry on and finish anything you're involved in.
SQUARE	You may be under a lot of stress at this time, which could cause you to be very tense and nervous. Your impulsive behavior may cause you a lot of unnecessary problems. Keep your temper under control at all times. There is a tremendous desire for changes now just for the sake of change. Check everything twice or three times before you make any changes and make sure that they are practical.
TRINE	A project you have been working on for years may be brought to a successful conclusion. This is a good time for speculation or gambling. Any new friendship formed at this time will become very reliable and rewarding to you. A very good time to start a serious study program. An unexpected change brought about under this aspect will be very beneficial for you.
OPPOSITION	NEVER HAPPEN IN THIS LIFE.

TRANSIT SATURN

KEYWORDS FOR SATURN

POSITIVE	NEGATIVE
TEACHES, CONTROLS STEADIES	TROUBLE DUE TO OLDER PEOPLE, ADMINISTRATORS OR PEOPLE IN AUTHORITY
ADDED RESPONSIBILITIES	FATHER OR HUSBAND
OLDER PEOPLE'S HELP	DOUBTS, ANXIETIES, APPREHENSIONS, UNCERTAIN FEARS
ADMINISTRATORS OR PEOPLE IN AUTHORITY	RASH SPEECH
PRACTICAL ACCOMPLISHMENTS	DEPRESSIONS
ENDURANCE	PESSIMISM
THRIFT	CHRONIC HEALTH PROBLEMS
TACT	ACCIDENTS
CAUTIOUS	LOSS OF MONEY
SELF CONTROL	LACK OF CONCENTRATION
PATIENCE	BAD FOR MARRIAGES
PLUMBERS	PARTING OF LOVED ONES AND FRIENDS
GARDNERS	LOSS OF PRESTIGE AND HONOR
FARMERS	LONLINESS AND SELF PITY
LANDLORDS	LOSS OF INCOME AND POVERTY
GOOD CONCENTRATION	
THOUGHTFUL	
INCREASES CREDIT	
POPULARITY AND ESTEEM	
SUCCESS	
GOOD JUDGEMENT	

TRANSIT SATURN IN THE HOUSES

HOUSES

1. Your life seems to slow down in all areas. This position could cause depressions, moodiness and many frustrations. Your health may be bad. Be extra careful of your health problems. You may start to learn to do things in a new way. There may be many added responsibilities in your life now. This position may cause a reduction of weight. This could make you cautious and timid.

2. A loss of income or reduction of income may cause you to completely overhaul your financial plans. This is a good time to make plans for the future. You will have to develop patience in regard to financial problems. You'll find that you will have to work harder for the same income. Stay away from all "get rich" schemes.

3. This is a good time to finish all old plans or any forms of communications. You may have to settle any old difficulties that you may have had in the past with sisters, brothers or neighbors. This position may cause delays and disappointment concerning your plans or schemes. Short trips may be very depressing, delayed or troublesome. You may find that you will have trouble with any studies you may want to start.

4. This may bring on added responsibilities in connection with domestic affairs. You may take on the responsibility of supporting one of the parents. Some may sell the old home and buy a larger one for the purpose of investment. Very good time to bring old projects to conclusion and to begin new ones.

5. All speculation or investment should be made with the purpose of long-term gains. You may find that you will have trouble getting your creative ideas across to others. Your children may demand more responsibility or cost you more money at this time. You may break off a current love affair and become attracted to a more mature person. Don't speculate, gamble or get involved in any "get rich" schemes. This is a poor time to borrow or loan your children money.

6. Be very careful with your health; at the first sign of any illness, consult your doctor. You may change your wardrobe to more dark tints or hues, or be inclined to buy clothing which is more conservative. The same amount of work may cause you to be fatigued or tired. If you quit your present job, you may have trouble finding another. A job acquired now could be very boring and tiresome. Many old chronic health problems may crop up.

7. You may marry at this time, not for love, but because you may feel it's time to settle down and assume more responsibility. Some old friend may come back into your life at this time. Competition in business may become stronger and cause you much worry and anxiety. There may be many delays or disappointments in regard to contracts having to do with business. Make sure that you read all the fine print in every contract you might wish to sign. If there are any afflictions in the seventh house in the natal chart, there may be much trouble in partnerships and marriages.

8.   The partner's money sources may be curtailed at this time. There-
      fore, you can't expect any financial help from the partner. An in-
      surance policy may mature at this time and you may receive it as a
      legacy, but no large amount. If there's any affliction in the 8th
      house in the natal chart, this may cause problems regarding other
      people's money and income tax. This also can cause health problems.
      You could become very interested in some occult subject.

9.   May become very interested in studying philosophy and religion.
      This could cause you to write to some publisher about a book you
      may have written. This position could cause lawsuits or divorces if
      there is any affliction in the 9th House in the natal chart. Many
      students drop out of college because they are so bored or depressed.
      This is a very poor time for any long distance traveling.

10.   Saturn in good aspect will bring honor and fame but if afflicted it
      could cause disgrace and dishonor. You may become very ambitious
      at this time. You may encounter many obstacles or disappointments
      because of those in authority. Your profession may cause many re-
      strictions in your domestic affairs. This also could bring on added
      responsibility because of one of the parents.

11.   A friend needing help may bring on added responsibility. This
      position could cause your application for membership in a society or
      club to be rejected. Wait until Saturn leaves this house before re-
      applying. There may be a loss of income from your profession or
      there may be a substantial increase in income from the profession.
      Your hopes and desires may be delayed, thus causing anxiety and
      depression. Some older and more mature people may assist you in
      some special area of your life. Saturn may hinder you but he is
      helping you to build a firm and more solid foundation for the future.

12.   Saturn in this house could cause many misunderstandings with those
      in positions of authority. You may also lose old friends. This
      position usually causes a person to desire to withdraw from the pub-
      lic and re-evaluate their position in life. The desire for seclusion is
      very strong at this time. Afflictions to Saturn here could cause bad
      health problems and a possibility of confinement to an institution.
      Many immature people at this time will be inclined toward self-pity.
      Many will resort to taking drugs or drinking alcohol to stimulate
      themselves. You may take on some sort of research project or
      others will become involved in helping those confined to some sort
      of institution. If you find yourself needing advice, this is a good
      time to turn to older and more experienced people for help.

TRANSIT SATURN ASPECTS

SATURN TO MOON

CONJUNCT   This could be a very depressing time for you emotionally and seems to slow down your ability to earn money. There will be more work and responsibility attached to any money earned at this time. This is a very good time to put your financial program on a more substantial basis. This particular aspect could cause much trouble with the wife and mother. Your feelings are easily hurt at this time. May have trouble with relatives in the home. This aspect could cause women to have very bad health problems.

SEXTILE   You may have an excellent opportunity to invest in some good real estate project. This is an excellent time to start a savings account. The domestic affairs and the home life are more settled now. This is an excellent time to get married.

SQUARE   You may be very depressed and prone to many tearful episodes. You may be very moody and brood a lot because things are not going the way you want them. You may become very ambitious and have a tendency to force your will on others. You may become very selfish and suspicious and cause people to reject you. This aspect could cause old chronic health problems to flare up. This is a very poor financial time. This is not the time to do any speculations or to invest in real estate. Any accomplishments brought about now will be the result of your working four times as hard for it. There will be many delays and disappointments.

TRINE   Your serious and responsible attitude could attract to you people, older and more mature, who will help you to attain your goals. Very good time to invest in real estate, buy a home or speculate in older firms. This is a good time to take up some serious studying because your concentration is very good. This aspect could indicate a promotion in your profession or on the job. A very good time to change work or to start a new job. The public is more receptive at this time.

OPPOSITION   This could be a time of much self pity. Your parents may be having domestic problems which are very depressing to you. An old girl friend may come back into your life. Your mother or wife may be ill at this time. This aspect could possibly cause a divorce. You may become extremely ambitious at this time.

SATURN TO MERCURY

CONJUNCT   This may be a very serious time for you. The only things you may be interested in are the serious or practical aspects of life. May receive some sort of depressing or disappointing communications. Your memory or power of concentration may be very poor at this time. You may have trouble with your voice and be plagued with chest colds. May have many worries and anxieties due to your negative attitude about life.

SEXTILE   This aspect could give you the opportunity to start a new job or new project with a good solid foundation. You may find at this time that you are able to communicate with older people easier. You are more optimistic and cheerful. This could be a good time to take short trips.

SQUARE   You could be involved in traffic jams and accidents, causing you to have transportation problems. You could be very sloppy at work or become a perfectionist at work, causing you trouble with co-workers and associates. You may have trouble trying to solve your problems because you're trying to solve them with old and obsolete methods. You may have many little irritating problems on short trips. May have many foul ups with reservations or time schedules. You could become very secretive or closed mouth. You may have a tendency to gossip at this time. You may have a nervous breakdown due to over work. This is a very poor time to sign any contract having to do with business. If you're a salesman, you may have trouble selling. Don't start any new project under this aspect. People seem to be forever missing their appointments with you.

TRINE   This is a favorable time to sign contracts for a long time benefit. Your concentration is very good now and you would be very good at detail work. Business appears to be steady and reliable. This is an excellent time to buy a dependable car. People are very punctual about keeping their appointments with you.

OPPOSITION   You seem to have trouble making up your mind about anything at this time. Those in authority appear to be opposing you at every turn. You may miss a very good opportunity because you will have trouble deciding about it.

SATURN TO VENUS

CONJUNCT   The key word appears to be "SADNESS". There probably will be a feeling of dejection and rejection from those you love. Your feelings are easily hurt and this may cause you to do a lot of brooding. You may go through many moods of depression. The loss of money or a position of responsibility may rest heavily on your shoulders.

SEXTILE   You may be very creative in a practical way. You may become more involved socially with older people. Tend to become more interested in serious recreational enjoyment. You may remodel or remake old things so they will look new again.

SQUARE   You may become interested in getting married for money and social position. You may find that you will have to make some kind of compromise that is not emotionally satisfying. You may become very disappointed with an older male friend or become separated from your wife. You could become very possessive and jealous at this time. You could become very fearful for your loved ones and about your personal security. You may have financial problems because you have spent too much on social events or luxuries. Your feelings are easily hurt at this time and you may brood over the slightest insult. Everything said or done is taken too personally. You may become very sloppy about your appearance and dress.

TRINE   Older people are enjoyable at this time. You may receive a visit or message from an old friend you haven't seen in a long time. You may receive a small raise at work or a slight promotion. Your attire is more conservative at this time.

OPPOSITION   You may experience many moods and depression because those close to you don't show their appreciation of you. You may be criticized at this time by older people because of your superficial or negative attitude. May indicate a social gathering you attend that you don't enjoy.

SATURN TO SUN

CONJUNCT   You may take everything too personally and seriously at this time. Don't let your pride cause you trouble with others. This may bring on more responsibility at work and with your parents. Old chronic health problems may flare up now. You may have physical collapse due to over work and worry.

SEXTILE   Your concentration and judgement is much better now. This is a good time to make a favorable impression with those in authority of the boss because of your serious attitude. Your health is improved at this time.

SQUARE   There may be financial losses. Business ventures may be failing. Those in authority may appear to be against you. It is a very unfavorable time to begin any new project or new business. You may become too aggressive at this time and cause older people to resist your efforts. Your health and vitality may be very low at this time. This would be an excellent time for a complete physical check-up. This is a very stressful time.

TRINE	This is a very favorable time for forming friendships with older people. This is a good time to change your line of work or to change jobs. This is an excellent time for increases in your income. This is a particularly favorable time to invest in some kind of real estate project for a long time increase. Your health and physical strength will be much improved. This is a good time to ask favors or for promotions from those in authority.
OPPOSITION	It seems like every obstacle in the world is being placed in your way by superiors, older friends or bosses. You may become very secretive and pessimistic. Your self confidence is at a low point now. Your physical strength and vitality are at their lowest. You may be torn between recreation and work. This is a very stressful time.

SATURN TO MARS

CONJUNCT	Your pep and enthusiasm are at their lowest peak. This could cause you to become very lazy. This could bring many muscle spasms. You may find yourself very nervous and irritable. Your attitude may become very rebellious and offensive to those around you. May become very hard nosed and cruel at this time.
SEXTILE	You may find that you can use your aggressiveness in a more positive way. You will be more patient with those that are less energetic than you, especially older men. You can get more done now with less physical activity.
SQUARE	This aspect causes a lot of carelessness and speed which could cause you many accidents. You may feel others are very abusive to you or you may become very abusive to others. Some of the older men may feel sexually impotent. You could become very sadistic or cruel at this time. This is a very poor time to change your line of work or job. You may become very impulsive one minute and very cautious the next. This is a very nerve-racking aspect due to a lot of emotional instability.
TRINE	Your physical strength and determination are very high now. Watch that you don't offend others because of your ambition and aggressiveness. This is an excellent time to start a project that needs a lot of physical strength and activity. Your health is much better now.
OPPOSITION	You are so active physically that you appear to be tired all the time. Your judgement is not very good at the present time because of your impulsiveness. May be extremely impatient because things are not going fast enough to suit you. You may loose in business because of this impatient attitude. You may have many muscle spasms due to too much physical activities.

SATURN TO JUPITER

CONJUNCT There may be many worries and anxieties about your financial program. Everything seems to come to a stand still at this time. This is an excellent time to get rid of all old worthless things in your life. This aspect could cause a reduction or loss of money in your income.

SEXTILE You will benefit the most at this time by finishing all old projects. Take care of routine matters and don't start any new financial deals. This could bring you dividends from an old insurance policy or some old contracts.

SQUARE You could lose in business or any new endeavors that you may try. Watch finances because you could become over-optimistic and over-expand and lose the entire bundle. This is a bad luck period. Wait until later to do any investing. Your expenses in business may be very high at this time. You may have to use your savings to pay old bills.

TRINE You may receive an inheritance or legacy from an older person now. Business will improve. This is an excellent time to start any new financial program. This is a good time to change jobs or to start a new business. Your judgement concerning any type of investment now is very good. This is a good time for students to start back to college.

OPPOSITION You may be demoted or lose prestige with older people. There is an indication of reduction in the income or losses in business. Any legal matters you are involved in may be settled against you. You may have trouble in making decisions at this time because your judgements seem to be faulty.

SATURN TO SATURN

CONJUNCT The key word is "NEW STARTS". This aspect could mean a rise to success and fame. Your health and vitality may be low. You may have to make very important decisions concerning your future. You may find that you will have to rid your life of old worthless things and this could cause you some emotional upset because of your emotional attachment. You may come to realize that you're getting older, or just plain old.

SEXTILE Older people or those in authority will become more interested in your progress. There may be added responsibiltiy at work but your pay will increase accordingly. You may receive a pay raise or a promotion because of past work record.

SQUARE	This is definitely not the time to start any type of dental work. Wait until later. You may receive extra responsibility at work without any extra pay. Your job or work may become a drudge and boring and you may want to quit. Don't become too discouraged or depressed about your efforts. Your business or your income may be so reduced that you will have to reorganize your financial program. Your health may suffer from some old chronic ailments or you may become subject to frequent colds or congestion of the chest.
TRINE	Prepare yourself for a long steady haul or start a project that will take time to complete. This aspect will make you very serious and responsible. This is an excellent time to get a physical check-up; be sure to listen to the doctor's advice.
OPPOSITION	This usually means a turning point in your career. This period can be very beneficial or very adverse. Success in business or career is likely to be eliminated. Make all your plans or ideas very practical. Your lack of self confidence can cause much nervousness and tension. A project started many years ago can be completed at this time.

SATURN TO URANUS

CONJUNCT	Old problems or conditions may unexpectedly be brought to an end. Drive carefully and don't travel by air because this is a strong accident aspect. You may have violent temper tantrums at this time if you don't control it. This also could bring unexpected fame and honors. There may be some great changes going on within your life. You may be torn between the old and the new.
SEXTILE	Your creative ideas concerning work will be very original and practical. Your insight and intuition may be very accurate at this time. You may be capable of concentrating very intently and for a long period of time. This could help you to accomplish much.
SQUARE	This aspect could cause an unexpected loss of prestige and honor, due to being aggressive or argumentive. You may use too much force in your approach to everything and cause those around you to be very hostile toward you. This aggression could cause you to be separated from a partner and old friends. You may be too impatient for your own good. Being rude or too abrupt with your boss could cause you to be fired. You may become extremely ambitious at this time and cause friends or those in authority to be against you. you.

TRINE   You seem to be able to revamp old ideas and make them
              appear like new ones. This is an excellent time to bring old
              problems to a satisfactory conclusion. This is a good time
              to deal with insurance companies or banks. You'll be able
              to use your creative and unique ideas to settle old business
              problems.

OPPOSITION   Those in high positions seem to be opposing you at work.
              This is a time when you may lack self-confidence about your
              creative ability, which could cause you to become very de-
              pressed. You may become very malicious or treacherous
              with anyone not in agreement with you. Your behavior may
              become very erratic and unpredictable.

SATURN TO NEPTUNE

CONJUNCT   You must make all of your ideas or plans very practical.
              Some may have trouble with reoccurring dreams that may
              be distressing and disturbing. You may become very appre-
              hensive about business or personal matters. There is a defin-
              ite lack of self confidence at this time.

SEXTILE   This aspect could cause you to be satisfied with things as
              they are. You are confident in relating to others. You could
              have some favorable things happen to you in regard to
              institutions.

SQUARE   This is a poor time to sign contracts. If you do, make sure
              you read all the fine print. Don't get involved in any "get
              rich" schemes. Don't rely on publicity because it can be
              very disappointing. Be very practical with all of your invest-
              ments at this time. Don't let your idealistic desires cause
              you to be impractical. Don't buy anything sight unseen.

TRINE   This could make you very practical in all of your creative
              endeavors. This is an excellent aspect for speculating or
              gambling. You may find yourself interested in studying
              some occult subject. Your sleeping is much more restful at
              this time.

OPPOSITION   There may be a very strong desire for reform, but those you
              are trying to reform may have other ideas. Those in high
              positions do not understand your high ideals. Doubts and
              fears plague you now.

SATURN TO PLUTO

CONJUNCT   You may become very disillusioned or discontented with Status Quo. If you try to make any permanent changes you will find yourself restricted by Status Quo or authority figures, or older people. There may be traffic accidents or fires that are started in odd ways that are hard to explain. You may be very doubtful about things going on around you at this time.

SEXTILE   This is a very good time to get involved in a research project of some sort. This aspect may bring an old friend back into your life, who has changed very drastically. You may become involved in a new intense love affair that is beneficial for you. This would be an excellent time to look into a new investment opportunity. You may want to pool your money with another for future gains.

SQUARE   Any anti-social behavior you feel may be demonstrated by you in a violent way. This is not a good aspect or good time for changes, but you may have changes forced on you by circumstances beyond your control. You may become involved in some type of crusade. Don't borrow or lend money under this aspect.

TRINE   This aspect could strengthen your deliberation, ambition and determination. You may feel you could do anything that you set out to do. Your finances will be improved under this aspect. This is a good time to speculate or gamble. You could profit by investing in real estate at this time.

OPPOSITION You may feel you're being imposed on by the establishment, but you will feel hesitant about doing anything about this. You may tend to become a rebel without a cause or have trouble figuring out just what you are rebelling about. You could become very fearful or doubtful about life in general. Vague fears plague you.

TRANSIT JUPITER

KEYWORDS FOR JUPITER

POSITIVE

INCREASES; ABUNDANCE
OPTIMISM
MIDDLE AGE PEOPLE
SPORTSMEN
PUBLISHERS

CLERGYMEN
TRIAL LAWYERS; LAW SUITS

SUCCESS IN CONTACT WITH
PEOPLE; ACHIEVEMENTS
UNDERSTANDING;
COMPASSIONATE
LUCK
MONEY
TOLERANCE

PROSPERITY; HONOR &
FAME
DOCTORS
GOOD JUDGEMENT: HONEST
JOVIAL
GENEROUS
POPULAR
BANKERS
CLOTHING, MEN'S
DISTANT COMMUNICATION
INHERITANCE

NEGATIVE

OVER EXPANSIVE
OVER SPENDS
MISJUDGEMENT
PEOPLE MISJUDGE YOU
LOSSES IN SPECULATION OR
GAMBLING
BAD IIMING
LOSSES IN BUSINESS OR
FINANCES
UNPOPULAR

LOSSES IN A LAWSUIT

INTOLERANT
UNSYMPATHETIC
ILL HEALTH DUE TO OVER
INDULGENCE
BLOOD DISEASES

TOO GENEROUS

TRANSIT JUPITER IN THE HOUSES

HOUSES

1. In this position Jupiter increases the weight, improves the health, increases your vitality and makes you more optimistic. An excellent time to start any new project or program. Many excellent opportunities may come your way through your association with those in authority. Your judgement is excellent at this time. Very good luck period.

2. Money seems to fall out of the clouds into your lap without any effort on your part. This will be a very lucky time for you financially. You could spend too much money because you may believe this luck will last forever. You could become too extravagant. You could have many speculations that are successful.

3. This would be an excellent time to seek promotions or increase your income. You will have more enjoyable times with your relatives. Many enjoyable short trips. This would be a good time to write a short story or book. You are more receptive to your relatives' plans and ideas.

4. Very favorable time for you to invest in some sort of real estate. Be an excellent time to remodel or improve your home. You have more enjoyable social affairs in your home. Your domestic affairs are more pleasurable. You could enjoy visiting with the parents. This is a good time to solve some old domestic problem to everyone's satisfaction.

5. You may be very successful in all of your speculations or investments. This is an excellent time to invest in new progressive enterprises. You may enjoy yourself more in your recreational activities. This is a good time for an enduring love affair. You become very interested in children's educational program. Those married at this time may increase their family.

6. You may be capable of doing a great amount of work without feeling any physical strain. Your association with your co-workers or employees is more pleasurable. Your health seems to improve without any effort on your part. This may increase your weight. Good time to change jobs with the ideas of looking for a more permanent one.

7. This is a good time to get married. This would be an excellent time to form a partnership with someone you trust. You will have many opportunities to overcome your competitors. You may sign business contracts with good results. Any public appearance you may make will be successful.

8. You and your partner may combine your finances with good results. This could be a good time to take out an insurance policy. May receive a legacy from a relative or friend. You can get credit without any special effort. Your marriage partner may receive a promotion or raise.

9. You may become very interested in studying philosophy, religion or some scientific subject. Long trips are taken with good results. Your relations with the in-laws are improved. This could be a good time to get married. This is an excellent opportunity to settle a lawsuit. Very good tome to send your book to a publisher, or for a student to start to college.

10. You may receive honors and success in your profession. This is an excellent time to ask those in authority for favors. A very good time to start a business. Favorable relationships with parents. This is a good position for social and domestic affairs.

11. Very favorable to meet influential people that belong to clergy, legal profession or foreign services. Your hopes and desires may be fulfilled at this time. This is an excellent time to join clubs, organizations or societies. A good time to form enduring friendships.

12. This aspect will help you to overcome secret enemies or those who have been plotting against you. You will probably seek more solitude. Banking may play a prominent role for some. A secret love affair may be carried on without anyone finding out. Ranching or cattle business may interest some. You may volunteer to work in some sort of an institution. This aspect may help some to get out of the institution to which they have been confined.

TRANSIT JUPITER ASPECTS

JUPITER TO MOON

CONJUNCT

This could bring favorable social affairs, also makes for compatibility concerning domestic affairs. Don't get involved with extravagant people. This is an excellent time to take a vacation. You may meet an important woman. Your relationship with your mother, sister or wife is very enjoyable.

SEXTILE

Don't jump to any conclusions without all the facts. Don't make any snap judgement because you may miss some of the facts. Don't let your emotions interfere with any of your decisions. You may gain through your friends, organizations and the public.

SQUARE

You may become too extravagant. Your wife may take a trip now. A woman friend may cause you a great deal of expense or anxiety. You may have many domestic upsets. Don't gamble or speculate at this time because you are apt to lose. Don't lend your children any money at this time as you may not get it back.

TRINE

The health of the family is excellent at this time. This is a lucky aspect as far as finances are concerned. This could also improve your social affairs. Some important woman could help you improve your finances. Good relations now with female relatives, mother and wife.

OPPOSITION

Don't speculate or gamble under this aspect, you could lose because your judgement is faulty. Put your money into savings bonds or promising real estate deals. Don't overwork. You may find yourself being opposed by female relatives, mother or wife. Don't expand your business now.

JUPITER TO MERCURY

CONJUNCT

Do not dodge obligations of long-standing. Keep relaxed and calm at all times. A good time to travel or go into business. Your mind may be over-confident or too optimistic. Be very practical under this aspect. Don't trust to luck.

SEXTILE

This is a good time to solve any old problems or dispose of any obstacle that may be in your way to success. Your thinking and attitude are more optimistic and your judgement is very sound at this time.

SQUARE You may make impulsive decisions and make mistakes. In your haste, you may not get all the facts. This could cause many emotional upsets due to little irritating phone calls received, letters, or people missing appointments with you. You may have many misunderstandings with others because you assume they understand you, when they don't. It's a poor time to sign any contracts. You may have trouble with younger men under this aspect.

TRINE Your communication will be improved under this aspect. This could give gains in small financial deals. You are more agreeable, calmer, relaxed and optimistic with this aspect. An excellent time to take short or long trips. People are more receptive of you now. Your contacts with younger men is improved at this time.

OPPOSITION You probably have a difficult time in making any kind of decisions at this time. Very poor time to do any kind of traveling. This aspect may separate you from people, especially your friends. You may become over optimistic and unrealistic. Idealistic ideas receive unfavorable response from those in authority because they probably lack practical goals.

JUPITER TO VENUS

CONJUNCT This is a favorable aspect to start a business or to get married. The public at this time is very receptive. You may receive many invitations to weddings. This could make all your social affairs very enjoyable. You may gain weight under this aspect.

SEXTILE This is an excellent aspect for business or social success. Brings much happiness in relationship to your marriage. This will improve your finances and social affairs.

SQUARE Your finances may suffer because you could become too extravagant with your spending. You may spend too much on social affairs, clothing, jewelry or luxury items. You may receive more invitations to social functions than you could possibly attend. Over-indulgences could cause your health to suffer. You could become very selfish now.

TRINE You are more considerate, understanding, broad-minded and liberal and are more willing to listen to both sides of the story. This is a good-luck period. You will have more success in business and your romances or love affairs. Your marriage will go smoother at this time.

OPPOSITION You had better watch your diet because you'll probably be craving rich and sweet foods. This could possibly cause impure blood. This period may cause a divorce or unhappiness in your marriage or can cause broken romances. Your over-indulgences in the past could cause ill health now. Financial losses are possible.

JUPITER TO SUN

CONJUNCT

This is a very favorable time to associate with influential people. Your health is good and you have a very optimistic attitude toward life. This is a good time to start any new project. Your social life could improve. This is a good time to take a trip for business or pleasure.

SEXTILE

This is an excellent time for business or any legal matterss you may need to tend to. This would be a very good time to butter up the boss for positive rewards. Your plans may be carried out without any extra efforts because people are very receptive to you at this time.

SQUARE

This aspect could cause you to become too aggressive or too impulsive. Be very honest and above-board in all of your contact with people. Don't over indulge in rich, sweet foods or drink alcoholic beverages to excess. You may have financial losses if you don't curb your extravagant spending. This is not the proper time to present any new idea or plans to the boss or those in authority because they are not receptive at the present time. Wait until later. You may have misunderstanding with husband or father.

TRINE

You're more sincere, understanding, sympathetic and compassionate with those who have troubles. You can make excellent progress in your financial gains. Your relationship with those in authority is very favorable, also with father or husband. You may be promoted or get a raise in pay. This is an excellent time to start a job or to get a new one.

OPPOSITION

Don't let yourself get too involved in other people's problems. This could bring on temporary separations in love affairs or romances due to circumstances beyond your control. The males in your life may be opposing what you're trying to do.

JUPITER TO MARS

CONJUNCT

You may have a strong tendency to be too extravagant at this time. This would be a good time to watch your finances very carefully. You may become so involved in physical activities that your health may suffer. Slow down and relax.

SEXTILE

This is a good period for business or any legal matters that need clearing up. Curb your tendency to over-do at the present time. Be very practical in everything you do. All your efforts will be rewarded.

SQUARE — You are too aggressive and impulsive. Your impulsiveness may interfere with your judgement. Get all the facts before you make any decisions. You could over-indulge in rich foods and alcoholic beverages, which could cause adverse effects on your health. You may suffer or lose money because of carelessness and impulsiveness. You are so impatient that you may aggravate those close to you.

TRINE — This is a lucky period for you in regards to finances and income. You're more understanding, compassionate and considerate now. You have a tremendous amount of energy and enthusiasm. Slow down and relax. Your judgement can be very accurate at this time.

OPPOSITION — The people you may be trying to help may turn on you because you are interfering too much in their problems. You may become too aggressive and argumentive and cause people to resent you. You may become very impatient with those who are slower than you.

JUPITER TO JUPITER

CONJUNCT — This is an excellent time to wind up all old business problems and to take care of legal problems. Some hope or desire you have had for years may be realized at the present time. Others may help you toward your goals.

SEXTILE — This is a good time to help a friend in need. Your judgement is very good. By being yourself you will be able to weather any unpleasant period. You are more optimistic now.

SQUARE — Your income may be improving but your expenses are much higher than the extra income. This could cause you trouble with your budget. Your enthusiasm and impulsiveness may interfere with your accuracy in judgement. This is a very bad time to start any new project.

TRINE — This is an excellent time to submit your book to a publisher. This is also a good time to advertise to increase your business. If you have a lawsuit pending, this could be a good time to settle favorably. A very lucky time. Could get good results in speculation or gambling. You're energetic, enthusiastic and in excellent health.

OPPOSITION — This aspect could be a combination of good and bad. You may become so enthusiastic about some area of your life that you ignore everything else. You may find that middle age males are opposing you. You may have to really sell yourself before anyone will listen to you.

JUPITER TO SATURN

CONJUNCT

This would be an excellent time to approach the boss with a request for a favor or a promotion. Your relationship with older people is much better. This is an excellent time to invest in real estate for long term gains. There could be a substantial gain in your income.

SEXTILE

This would be an excellent time for all investments involving old and established firms. Your concentration is very good now and it would be beneficial for you to study a serious subject. You have a tendecny to be very serious and practical at this time.

SQUARE

The key word here is "BAD LUCK". You may find a large reduction in your finances and income. Business may be lousy. Don't borrow or lend money at this time. Your timing and judgement may cause you trouble with older people or those in authority. You may receive more responsibility concerning elderly people. There may be an argument or disagreement with your father.

TRINE

There should be a steady increase in your finances or income but nothing spectacular. A good time to invest in real estate or an old established firm. You're more optimistic at this time and your health could improve.

OPPOSITION

You may separate from a partner or receive a divorce from your marriage partner. Older people may be opposing you. Everything seems to have slowed down to a crawl. Your lack of self confidence may make it difficult for you to make a decision about anything.

JUPITER TO URANUS

CONJUNCT

You may experience a strong desire for complete independence or freedom. This could increase your creativeness or ingenuity. There may be unusual opportunities offered you at the present time. Be careful that you don't over-expand in business or in any new investments.

SEXTILE

You may become interested in studying unusual occult subjects, such as Astrology or religion. You may have more opportunities to demonstrate your executive abilities.

SQUARE

You may unexpectedly change your religious views or philosophical approach to life. May become interested in studying unusual unorthodox subjects, such as black magic. This could bring about much tension and nervousness which could interfere with your sleep or relaxation. You may try short cuts that are not practical because you tend to be too impatient. This is a poor time to speculate or gamble. Unexpected financial losses may occur.

TRINE   You may receive unexpected promotion or honor because of
               your past work record. Your insight and judgement are very
               good during this epriod. Don't become over confident.

OPPOSITION   You may find unexpected competition with older males.
               Competition in business may be so great that you could lose
               money or income. Your impulsiveness or your over optim-
               istic attitude may interfere with your judgement. Be very
               practical in everything you do. You could have unexpected
               lawsuit or legal action.

JUPITER TO NEPTUNE

CONJUNCT   You may feel super sensitive to other people. Your dreams
               will be numerous and probably very prophetic. This is an
               excellent time to study anything that is creative, such as
               music or painting. Don't get involved in "get rich" schemes
               or projects.

SEXTILE   Some hope or desire that you have had for years may materi-
               alize. Your intuition and hunches may be very accurate
               during this period, and your attitude is more optimisitc.

SQUARE   You should not get involved in any extreme religious cults
               or with any fanatical people. You may lose money and
               have problems trying to figure out how you did it. Don't
               get involved in any "get rich" schemes. The practical ap-
               proach is the best. Just sit tight until later. Your idealistic
               hopes and ideas may interfere with your better judgement.

TRINE   You may have an unexpected increase in your finances.
               Some creative ideas come to you in flashes. Your artistic
               talents may be developed easily during this period. This is a
               good time to take trips.

OPPOSITION   Many will be questioning their old ideas about religious
               beliefs. Others may resort to alcohol or drugs to escape
               from their personal problems. You could be deceived or
               cheated by friends or partners. Your judgement may be
               faulty at this time.

JUPITER TO PLUTO

CONJUNCT   You may find that you are getting rid of old and useless
               things in your life. This is a very good period for those en-
               gaged in religious activities, welfare or hospital work. Don't
               try to reform people who don't want to be reformed. Watch
               your diet very closely because you may gain a lot of weight.

SEXTILE	You may receive payments from other people that have been long overdue. An excellent time to begin any research project you're interested in. Very lucky period in your life.
SQUARE	You may find yourself becoming very selfish and demanding. There may be many people opposing you at this time. Immature people under this aspect have a tendency to become physically violent. You should pay off all old debts if possible. Don't begin any new credit accounts. The key word is "BAD LUCK". Your selfishness could interfere with your judgement.
TRINE	The key word is "LUCK". This is a favorable period for taxes, estates and research projects. It seems as though whatever you try to do, it comes out right. A very good time to study anything that pertains to higher education, philosophy or religion. Your judgement is excellent under this aspect.
OPPOSITION	You may be over optimistic at this time and this will cause you to fail in the things you're trying to do. You may feel like using physical force against those who are opposing you at the present time. Your over-expansive feeling that nothing could go wrong may cause you to overspend on social affairs or luxury items. This aspect is very bad time to take a trip. Stay home or be very careful if you do go.

TRANSIT MARS

KEYWORDS FOR MARS

POSITIVE	NEGATIVE
ENERGIZES	IMPULSIVE BEHAVIOR
YOUNG MEN	THREATS
SERVICE MEN	ACCIDENTS
ATHLETES; PHYSICAL ACTIVITY	ARGUMENTS AND QUARRELS
CREATIVE IDEAS	TEMPER FLARE UPS
COURAGE AND PHYSICAL STRENGTH	RESTLESS AND NERVOUS
IMPETUOUS	LOSSES IN FINANCES AND BUSINESS
BUYING AND SELLING	BURNS, CUTS, SCALDS & FEVERS
CONSTRUCTION; CARPENTERS	FIRES AND THEFTS
TRANSPORTATION	INJURIES
POLICE	OVERWORK
SOLDIERS	OVER PASSIONATE
DENTISTS; SURGEONS	BE CAREFUL OF DIET
SALES AND COMMISSIONS	NO OPERATIONS
ALCOHOLIC BEVERAGES	IMPULSIVE SPEECH
AMBITION	ANGER
BOLDNESS	DOMINEERING AND RASH
COOKS	IRRITABLE
ENTHUSIASM	DOMESTIC UPSETS
FOREHEAD	BLOOD POISONING

TRANSITING MARS IN THE HOUSES

HOUSES

1. You may become more ambitious, aggressive and determined. You may become very irritated because things are not moving fast enough, and you could have temper flare ups. Your judgement may be faulty at this time because you are so impulsive. You could cause others to resent you because you are trying to force your opinions on them. There may be accidents because you're in too big of a hurry.

2. You may increase your income but you will impulsively spend it faster than you can earn it. Don't start any credit accounts that will take you a long time to pay off. Be practical in your spending and you will be happier.

3. Don't take trips just to be moving around. This is a poor time to study or take classes because your mind is so active that you will have trouble concentrating and learning. Don't write or say anything that you may be sorry about later. You may have quarrels with brothers, sisters or neighbors. This could cause accidents on trips, so be more cautious at this time.

4. This position could cause fires and accidents in the home. There may be misunderstandings and arguments with parents in the home and this may cause you to move out of the parents' home. You may be involved in making decisions concerning your home life or matters relating to real estate. Don't make any impulsive decisions about any of the above-mentioned things.

5. You may make impulsive decisions concerning your love affairs, children, or you may have an extreme desire at this time to speculate or gamble. There is a strong desire to get so involved in some types of physical activities in your search for fun that you may over-do and injure your health. You will have many creative ideas, but you may have problems by trying to force these ideas on others. Make sure these creative ideas are very practical.

6. This position could cause extreme tension, nervousness and over-work. You'll probably be so energetic that you won't get enough rest and this could cause health problems. This would be an excellent time to look for a new job if the aspects are favorable but if adverse, don't do it. This could cause arguments with co-workers or the boss because of their out-spokenness. Keep a firm grip on your temper.

7. May be involved in enjoyable parties or social affairs with friends or your partner. This would be a good time to sign contracts that have been pending, if the aspects are good. Again, if the aspects are right, you could come before the public in some way.

8. You may want to take out an insurance policy or cancel one that you have. There may be trouble with partner's finances or with taxes. You may attend a function relating to the occult. Your physical sex drive may be very strong at this time. You could have an argument about a legacy.

9. Be very careful or you may have some arguments with your in-laws. Some legal matters or lawsuit that has been pending for a long time may be settled now. You may have a strong urge to take a long distance trip at this time, or you may receive some kind of communications from people from afar. This position could stimulate you in studying philosophy or religion. Some students may start back to college.

10. You will become very ambitious and have a strong urge to succeed at this time. The results will be according to the type of aspects that are operating. Don't let yourself become too tense or nervous because you may get too impatient with those who are slower than you. This could possibly cause some friction in your domestic affairs.

11. There may be many invitations from casual friends. You could become very involved in club or organizational functions. You are more popular with people attending social affairs. You will be more attracted to younger and more energetic people. You could possibly have many arguments with older friends.

12. This is an excellent time to check your plans and ideas before putting them into action. Don't let yourself become too impulsive. By being over active you may endanger your health. Secret enemies may make false accusations or try to make trouble by lying about you. You may be confined in a hospital for an operation. This is an excellent time to help those who are less fortunate.

TRANSIT MARS ASPECTS

MARS TO MOON

CONJUNCT

This could become a very emotional period. There will be many ups and downs pertaining to business and work. May make many short trips. This could be a very favorable time concerning relationships with females. Guard against fire damages and theft. Don't let your emotions interfere with your judgement.

SEXTILE

You may become emotionally involved with women. You should have many pleasant contacts with the public. Your health will seem to improve but this depends on the types of aspects. Your moods are very changeable.

SQUARE

You could be extremely impulsive and emotional now. These emotional changes could cause many temper tantrums. There could be arguments and disagreements with women, wife, or mother. Drive very carefully at this time because this is a good aspect for accidents due to carelessness.

TRINE

Your emotions are more stable at this time. Many pleasant public and social functions. You will enjoy the company of women, wife or mother. This usually is good for salesmen because they can deal with the public in a very tactful way.

OPPOSITION

In all forms of communications be very tactful. Think twice before you say anything and keep your temper under control at all times. Slow down your driving and be more careful. You may have many little irritating arguments with wife or mother.

MARS TO MERCURY

CONJUNCT

Don't be so argumentative, think twice before you speak or say anything. Don't be in such a hurry to get some place because this speed could cause you to get a speeding ticket or become involved in an accident. You could become very tense and nervous under this aspect. Read the fine print in all papers you have to sign. You will have trouble sleeping because you can't seem to turn off your thinking.

SEXTILE

You can think faster and clearer at this time. You may be able to impress someone in high places because of your ability to think fast and to make the right decisions. Make sure you answer all of your correspondences quickly and accurately.

SQUARE

You may receive some type of correspondence that will cause you to lose your temper. Don't make any decisions pertaining to finances until a later date. Your impulsiveness could influence your judgement so you would make the wrong decision and lose financially. Don't over work because this could affect your health.

TRINE   This is an excellent time to answer all types of correspondence. A very good time to take a trip for business or pleasure. You will be able to present your plans and ideas to others with ease. Excellent time to make decisions concerning your financial program for good results. Your judgement is very good at this time.

OPPOSITION   This aspect can cause tension and nervousness. Slow down and relax. You may find that some young man or the younger people are opposing you. Don't be impulsive in your speech because it could cause you to get involved in quarrels. This is a good time to control your temper. Don't over work because it could cause you to become physically exhausted.

MARS TO VENUS

CONJUNCT   You may become very popular and receive many invitations to social affairs. May be attractive to the opposite sex. You may become very extravagant and spend too much money on social affairs and luxuries. Your physical sex drive may be very strong at this time.

SEXTILE   You could become impulsively involved with the opposite sex. Your desire for fun may cause you to ignore your work. Don't let your emotions get you into trouble with women.

SQUARE   At this time you could be imposed on because of your generosity. You may become impulsively involved with a married woman. Watch your finances very carefully. Don't impulsively spend on social affairs, such as going out to expensive restaurants or night clubs. This is a poor time to make a decision about any financial programs. Wait until later.

TRINE   You will become involved in many enjoyable social affairs and parties. The opposite sex finds you very magnetic and attractive. You may be attracted to younger women at this time. Your love affairs and romances proceed very harmoniously. You are very tactful and considerate of other people. You find it very easy to earn money or sell people on your creative ideas. This is a very good aspect for the artist.

OPPOSITION   You may find that you will have many arguments with younger women around you. Your aggressive attitude may cause you to be separated from some younger sister or a younger woman. Your feelings appear to be super sensitive. You get your feelings hurt at the slightest little thing. You may lose financially because you will make decisions concerning your finances while you are upset. All the social affairs you attend may have everyone arguing or quarreling. You may become very extravagant at this time and spend money on luxuries that you can't afford.

MARS TO SUN

CONJUNCT   Your impulsiveness may cause your judgement to be faulty. Your tension and nervousness may cause you to lose your temper because eveyrone else seems to be moving so slow. This may give the impression of holding you back. You may have many contacts with males in your business. You may receive a promotion because of your energetic approach to your work.

SEXTILE   This aspect could increase your popularity with males, especially the men you work with. This could be an excellent time to look for a new job or to.change your profession. Those in high positions are more receptive to you now.

SQUARE   Your impulsiveness and aggressiveness could cause you to get into many arguments. Watch your tongue and your temper. You may be very successful at this time, but your over aggressiveness may cause those around you to resent you. Be more tactful and considerate and it will get you better results. Don't over work or it could affect your health in an adverse way.

TRINE   Your energetic and positive approach to your work will be noticed by those in authority and could earn you a promotion. Your aggressiveness is received by those around you in a positive way. You find that you can reach others by your sincerity and honesty. Your health is improved at this time.

OPPOSITION   It seems like everyone is opposing your plans and ideas, especially those in authority or males. Learn to listen and compromise and you'll have better results with your plans and ideas. Your tension, anger and nervousness may affect your health.

MARS TO MARS

CONJUNCT   Don't let your impulsiveness and aggressiveness get you into arguments. Watch your tongue and your temper. You may be very successful at this time, but your over aggressiveness may cause those around you to resent you. Be more tactful and considerate and it will get you better results. Don't over work or it could affect your health in an adverse way.

SEXTILE   Your judgement may be faulty because decisions made at the present time may be impulsively made. This could be an excellent period if you would relax more and not push others around.

SQUARE   You may become very angry because things are not moving
              fast enough for you. Trying to force the pace to speed up
              may cause you many arguments and cause people to reject
              you or reject your plans and ideas. Don't be so impatient
              with those slower than you. Don't do any impulsive spend-
              ing at this time. This aspect could cause fevers and accidents
              with fire or cutting tools. These accidents are usually
              caused by being in too much of a hurry and plain old
              carelessness.

TRINE   Your vitality is extremely high. At this time, you could
              accomplish anything physically that you wanted to but by
              over working you could cause yourself harm. This is an ex-
              cellent time to start new projects that need physical activity.

OPPOSITION   Curb your impatience. Don't try to buck city hall; you'll
              lose every time. All the males you come in contact with
              seem to be against you and everything you stand for. Don't
              make any impulsive decisions at this time about finances or
              work. This could cause you to become involved in some
              sort of physical violence.

MARS TO JUPITER

CONJUNCT   Your over optimistic attitude about your finances may
              cause you to become very extravagant in spending. You
              could become over confident and attempt to do something
              that would be impossible to accomplish. Your being over
              optimistic may cause your judgement to be faulty. Think
              twice before you do anything.

SEXTILE   Your business will run more smoothly at this time and your
              financial programs will increase. This is an excellent time
              to form a business partnership or to get married.

SQUARE   There could be unexpected financial expenditures that could
              drain your finances. Your extreme over confidence could
              cause your judgement to be faulty. Find out all the facts
              before you make a decision. You may become involved in
              some legal matters or a lawsuit. You may wish to get away
              from everything and everybody. This very definitely is a
              bad time to start any new business or project.

TRINE   This is a very lucky period. You will find that your business
              will improve and there will be an increase in your income.
              This aspect may cause you to want to buy some kind of
              machinery or a car. This is a favorable time for all legal
              matters. An excellent time to settle legal matters or lawsuits.
              A good time to take a trip for business or pleasure.

OPPOSITION   You may find that you will have a tendency to buy impulsively and your finances will suffer. Watch your budget very closely. Everyone and everything seems to go against you. If there is a lawsuit at this time, it may be settled against you. If you have any important decisions to make, try to put them off until later.

MARS TO SATURN

CONJUNCT   Don't plan a trip or take one because everything will seem to go against you. Everything in your life appears to come to a stand still and you can't seem to get anything moving. This could be a very frustrating time for you. You may have quarrels and arguments with elderly males or those in authority.

SEXTILE   You will begin to get results from all of your efforts. Keep your schedule and keep plodding away. You may not have any smashing successes but you will gradually succeed. Some older male or one of your superiors may help you to get the promotion that you deserve.

SQUARE   You will have to work harder and accept more and more responsibility without gaining anything financially. You may have many quarrels with older males or those in authority, or the boss. This argumentative attitude could cause you to be fired from the job. The tension and frustration that you are going through may affect your health in an adverse way. You might feel overly tired and worn out at this time.

TRINE   Your work and business will steadily advance. Your increase in income will grow steadily also. You find at this time you can get along and communicate with older males and superiors easier. Health is much better also. Could be a good time to help one of the parents.

OPPOSITION   You may be trying to go in two different directions at once. This could cause you to want to get away from it all. You may feel tired or exhausted all the time. You may feel very depressed or have many little vague fears. You may be very cautious and then too impulsive. Your automobile could give you unexpected problems and cost you money.

MARS TO URANUS

CONJUNCT   You may impulsively decide to toss away everything you
           have worked for and start in some other area of work. This
           could cause trouble in partnerships, marriages or with old
           friends. The tension and nervousness could cause you to
           have an uncontrollable temper at this time.

SEXTILE   Your determination and will power will help you to accom-
           plish whatever you have set out to do. A superior may un-
           expectedly help you get a promotion that you have been
           trying to get for months. You are very energetic and healthy
           at this time.

SQUARE   You could have unexpected accidents caused by your care-
           lessness. You could become involved in some sort of physi-
           cal violence due to your anger. This is very frustrating
           because the unexpected is throwing you off balance. You
           could possibly lose your job because of unexpected lay-off,
           or you could be fired because of your aggressiveness. You
           may feel that everyone is against you at this time.

TRINE   Your intuition could be very reliable at this time. You may
           have an unexpected promotion or an unexpected oppor-
           tunity to form a partnership with someone, which will help
           help you to gain financially. You are much more energetic
           your health is much better. You may become involved un-
           expectedly with the opposite sex.

OPPOSITION Don't let yourself be depressed or discouraged by temporary
           set backs. Don't let your tension and nervousness cause you
           to have sudden temper flare ups. You may become involved
           in a temporary love affair. Relax and rest to protect your
           health.

MARS TO NEPTUNE

CONJUNCT   This is a very confused period. This confusion could make
           you want to indulge in alcoholic beverages or to use some
           type of drugs. There appears to be much deception around
           you in business and work. Make sure you are honest in
           everything you do. People around you are forever promis-
           ing you things but don't expect them to carry out their
           promises.

SEXTILE   You may seem to be looking at the world through rose
           colored glasses. Don't be deceived at this time by appear-
           ances because things may not be what they appear to be.
           This would be an excellent time to develop your artistic or
           musical talents. You may become involved in drama or
           acting.

SQUARE   Don't tell your personal secrets to the public because some-
            one may use them against you. Your carelessness may cause
            you to have unexpected accidents. You may over indulge
            in alcoholic beverages or drugs which could endanger your
            health. Be extra careful if you are around water.

TRINE   You may find that you will have more creative ideas and
            plans. The study of philosophy or religion may interest
            you at the present time. You may have unexpected good
            luck in regards to your finances. You may become interested
            in developing your own psychic abilities.

OPPOSITION Watch your tongue because your emotions may cause you
            to say things that you will regret later. Don't over indulge
            in alcoholic beverages or drugs. Some male may be gossip-
            ing about you. This also could cause you to be involved in
            some sort of scandal.

MARS TO PLUTO

CONJUNCT   Be more tactful at this because an argument could cause
            a permanent separation between you and your partner
            Competitors and secret enemies may go to any length to get
            the best of you. Don't let yourself get overly aggressive.

SEXTILE   You are very energetic and your health is much better. You
            find that you can solve any of your problems with ease.
            This is an excellent time to start a new project that needs
            physical strength.

SQUARE   Don't let your aggressiveness provoke an argument. Your
            judgement may be very faulty at the present time because
            of your impulsiveness. Accidents could occur at this time
            because of carelessness. You may find that middle aged
            men are opposing you in what you are trying to do.

TRINE   This is an excellent time to get rid of all useless things in
            your life. Your health is much better than it has been. This
            is a good time to start a project that needs time to complete.
            This would be a good time to do some remodeling in your
            home because you have more energy and strength.

OPPOSITION You may become very impulsive and want to force things
            because they are not moving fast enough to satisfy you.
            You may become aware that someone is working against
            you behind your back. With a little cooperation from you,
            things could turn out much better. Watch your temper.

TRANSIT SUN

KEYWORDS FOR SUN

POSITIVE	NEGATIVE
MALES	LOSS IN FINANCES OR BUSINESS
SUPERIORS; AUTHORITY	LOSS OF PRESTIGE
HONORS AND FAME	ARROGANCE
GAINS IN FINANCES OR BUSINESS	EXCESSIVE PRIDE
VITALITY (ENERGY)	ILL HEALTH
LEADERSHIP	EXCESSIVE ENERGY
AMBITIONS ATTAINMENT	RESTLESSNESS
SELF CONFIDENCE	IMPATIENCE
RECOGNITION	GAMBLING
FATHER; HUSBAND	SPECULATING

TRANSIT SUN IN THE HOUSES

HOUSES

1. All of your personal affairs become very important to you. You may feel like you have more vim and vigor. This could make you feel very self confident. This is an excellent time to be sociable and ask favors of superiors or males in your life.

2. You may convince your superiors now that you should have a promotion or a raise. You become very involved in your plans regarding your financial program. You may become interested in buying new or different furniture for your house.

3. You may receive some sort of communication from a male relative. This would cause you to become interested in catching up on all of your correspondence. Your interest in writing could be stimulated; you may become interested in some type of educational classes or studying. This aspect could also bring about many short trips.

4. Your relationship with the males in the home is very favorable. This is a good time for all domestic affairs. You may become very interested in real estate. You may have an important male guest in the home or a surprise visit from your parents.

5. You will be able to put your creative ideas and plans across to others. You will enjoy children more and become very interested in their educational programs. You may become interested in speculation and gambling. You may become involved in social affairs or some sort of recreational affairs that are important to your career.

6. This will be good for your health. An excellent time to go on a diet. A male co-worker or associate may help you in some way. This would be a good time to look for a new type of work.

7. You may find that your partner or marriage partner is more cooperative. The public and close friends are more receptive to your creative ideas and plans. Some important people could help you to improve your business.

8. This position could help improve your partner's finances. You may receive a legacy or a tax refund at this time. You may become interested in an occult subject. You may buy an insurance policy or cash in the one you have now.

9. You may start planning a long distance trip or take one now. There may be some type of communication from your in-laws in another part of the country. You may come in contact with a lawyer or judge in regard to a legal matter. May become more interested in studying philosophy or religion. You may attend church more regularly now. May start college with this aspect.

10. Your superior or an important man may help you to improve your business or help you in your profession. You may become very interested in governmental affairs. This would be an excellent time to start your own business.

11. You may have more social contact with superiors or with important people. A friend may help you receive an important promotion. This would be a good time to join a club, society or organization. You may receive something that you have hoped and wished for.

12. You may become involved in a secret romance now. There may be an extreme desire to go into seclusion for a while. You may become interested or involved in some sort of institution. Avoid revealing any secrets about yourself because a secret enemy may use this information against you.

TRANSIT SUN ASPECTS

SUN TO MOON

CONJUNCT   Your energy and vitality are much stronger now. You may have many successful contacts with the public or with women. The finances should increase in your business.

SEXTILE   You can make a favorable impression on the public and the women around you. A woman in authority may offer you her help. Your domestic affairs are very pleasant at this time. Wife and mother are easier to get along with.

SQUARE   The business and the home may cause you many emotional upsets. If you work for a woman boss, you may have trouble with her at this time. Your emotional upheavals may upset your health. Mother, older sister or wife may give you a bad time now.

TRINE   You will have more pep and energy. Your emotions are more stable. This aspect could increase your income. You will enjoy public affairs with men and women more. This is an excellent time to take on added responsibilities for financial gains.

OPPOSITION   Your emotions are very unstable and could cause you to be very argumentative. Don't try to force your opinions on others. This emotional tension could cause health problems. There may be a financial loss. You may try to avoid responsibilities.

SUN TO MERCURY

CONJUNCT

This aspect stimulates the mental processes. You may have a desire to write or catch up on all of your correspondence. You could take a short trip for pleasure or business. You could make many small business deals.

SEXTILE

An excellent time to catch up on all paper work, clerical work or to sign any contracts. You may receive some good news in the mail or by phone. A good time to take short trips for pleasure or business. This is an excellent time to associate with younger people, especially younger men.

SQUARE

This aspect could cause you to worry about little things. The tension and nervousness may affect your health. May receive bad news in some form of communication. Don't take any short trips. Refrain from arguments or disagreements with others because this could cause them to resent you. Many disputes with younger men may occur.

TRINE

You may find at this time you can communicate with others, especially younger people, with ease. Your thinking will have a more serious trend now. The messages received will contain pleasant news. Your thinking and judgement are more accurate. Your health is much better.

OPPOSITION

Your thinking is being stimulated to the point that you have trouble turning it off. All mental jobs may be solved in half the usual time. You may find that you can express yourself very fluently. Finish all routine work. This is an excellent time to finish all outstanding projects. Don't sign any contracts without reading the fine print. Catch up on all correspondence.

SUN TO VENUS

CONJUNCT

This aspect has a tendency to increase your social activities. You may find yourself being drawn more and more to the company of the opposite sex. You should have a gain in your income or your business.

SEXTILE

An excellent time to buy the luxuries you have been wanting for some time. There should be a tremendous improvement in your social, business and home life. This could be an inspirational time for any artistic or creative activity.

SQUARE

You may have trouble with marriage partner or with your romances due to your own fickleness. May have to face the responsibilities that you have been ignoring. Don't let yourself become lazy or sloppy in your work or dress. Your feelings may be hurt easily.

TRINE   You will enjoy social affairs much more at this time and will become more involved in them. Friends will show their appreciation of you. Financial affairs seem to improve. Your health is much better. You may buy new clothes at this time without causing a loss in your budget.

OPPOSITION   You could go to an extreme now by getting too involved in parties and social affairs and this might cause your health to suffer and also might deplete your finances. This aspect could cause arguments with old friends or a lover. These arguments could cause a separation. You may cause trouble concerning your budget because you'll be spending too much on parties and social affairs. Don't give parties because everyone will seem too negative.

SUN TO SUN

CONJUNCT   This may be an over stimulating time. There will be a lot of tension and nervousness to control. This is the time to be more cautious; remember, haste makes waste. This aspect may make you dissatisfied with your work or your profession. Superiors may put pressure on you to do something that you may not want to do.

SEXTILE   Your friends become very important to you at this time. You will think more of their interests and they will be concerned about you and your activities.

SQUARE   You may resist those in authority, such as father, husband, boss or other important males in your life. Make sure that you control your temper at all times now. There is much tension and nervousness in your life. You may endanger your health by over work, because you're trying to get some release from this tension. Don't force anything, let everything flow at an even pace.

TRINE   Your health will improve at this time because there is less strife and tension around you. The authority around you will be more receptive of your creative ideas and plans. You will accept added responsibilities gracefully. Your business and work could improve now.

OPPOSITION   Your temper appears to have a short fuse. Tension and nervousness will cause you to have unexpected temper tantrum. Income from your business may suffer because you may have to pay old debts. All the males around you seem to be opposing you at this time, especially those in authority.

SUN TO MARS

CONJUNCT   You may become very ambitious at this time in all matters relating to your profession or work. Males or superiors may criticize you without just cause. Your health could suffer because you may over work.

SEXTILE   Now is the time to do any physical work that needs to be done but don't over-do. Your impatience and hurry may offend those around you and cause arguments and resentments. Have a little more patience with those who are slower in action than yourself.

SQUARE   Your speeding and impatience could cause you to have an accident. Don't let yourself become careless or tactless in relating to others. Don't sign any contracts relating to business or speculative projects because you could lose money on these deals now.

TRINE   Your health will improve under this aspect. This would be an excellent time to help a friend in need. Your relationship with males and those in authority will improve. You may get a promotion or raise because of your past efforts.

OPPOSITION Your creative ideas and plans may be opposed by males and those in authority. You may have many quarrels and misunderstandings at this time. Don't be careless or reckless in your driving because you may have an accident. This could be a very frustrating time for you.

SUN TO JUPITER

CONJUNCT   This is a very good aspect for dealing with superiors, business partners, associates and employers. This could bring about a promotion or get you a raise in pay. This is an excellent time to ask favors of a boss or supervisor.

SEXTILE   The key word here is "LUCK". This would be a good time to speculate or gamble. Also, a good time to expand your business. Don't become too optimistic because you may over expand and lose financially.

SQUARE   Bad luck seems to plague you in everything you attempt to do. You may lose in business or your expenses may increase, therefore, reducing your profits. Don't speculate under this aspect because your judgement appears to be faulty. You could be too optimistic at this time; be practical in everything you do.

TRINE	The key word is "GOOD LUCK". This would be an excellent time to expand your business and gain financially. It may appear that you can't make any mistakes in anything you do. Don't get carried away with your luck because this aspect doesn't last very long.
OPPOSITION	Your judgement may appear faulty because of your over optimistic attitude. Don't get upset if superiors appear to be opposing you; they are just checking on your ideas and plans to see if they are practical. Make sure all forms of communication are thoroughly understood by those with whom you are dealing.

SUN TO SATURN

CONJUNCT	Everything in your life appears to come to a stand still. There may be added responsibilities at work and with males but no raise in pay. This aspect could bring on depressions if there are any afflictions to Natal Saturn. You may feel like you have less vitality.
SEXTILE	There may be added responsibilities but you will get paid for them. This could bring results to a project you have been working on for a long time. These results usually relate to business or work.
SQUARE	This aspect usually is bad for your health and business. There could be a financial loss at this time. This may bring on depressions because of loss of money, bad health, or a loss of reputation. You could get fired under this aspect. Don't quit your job unless you are very sure the next job is much better.
TRINE	You will be able to get along better with older males, your father, or the boss. This is an excellent time to start a project requiring years to mature. You will get recognition or honor for your past work record. Excellent time to invest in a home or real estate.
OPPOSITION	Added responsibilities will bother you, but if you accept them, you will be rewarded at a later date. You may have to face many problems now that you had put off in the past. This could be a frustrating time for you and cause depressions and ill health. You may seem to be tired all the time or feel tired from the slightest physical activity.

SUN TO URANUS

CONJUNCT
There's a tremendous amount of willpower and determination. You will appear to shine in everything you do. This tremendous will power and magnetism will help you to succeed in business or in your profession. Your health is greatly improved under this aspect.

SEXTILE
Your creative ideas and plans will gain the approval of the boss or those in the position of authority. This would be an excellent time to increase your business or to ask the boss for a promotion.

SQUARE
There could be many unexpected arguments or disagreements with those in authority or the boss. Could cause a loss in business or cause you to unexpectedly get fired. There is a tendency to be in too much of a hurry which causes mistakes on the job. You will probably be so tense and nervous that it will affect your health in an adverse way. There could be many muscle spasms or teeth problems.

TRINE
You may become very involved in social affairs at this time. May unexpectedly be introduced to high officials in the government or high positions in large organizations. You may become very serious and ambitious. A good time to start a project that will take years to complete. Your health should be greatly improved at this time.

OPPOSITION
Extreme nervousness and tension could cause many disagreements with high officials or males. Don't let yourself become too aggressive because you may offend the ones who could help you in your career. Don't let your pride get the best of you. Be more flexible and compromise in everything you do and you will be rewarded.

SUN TO NEPTUNE

CONJUNCT
This aspect could cause extreme restlessness and vague fears. Don't let your imagination get carried away. Check everything you do twice to see if what you plan is practical. You could help those confined in institutions or patients in hospitals confined to their beds.

SEXTILE
This is an excellent time to express your creative and inspirational ideas and plans. This is a good time to participate in large groups. Also, an excellent time to start a self improvement program.

SQUARE
Your emotions and vague fears interfere with your judgment. This confusion could cause you to make mistakes. You could be deceived at this time by the boss, father, or a boy friend, or you could deceive one of them. This brings about confusing changes in your life that could affect your health. You may find that you have trouble sleeping or you may have terrifying dreams or nightmares while this aspect is in force.

TRINE	Your health should be better because there is less tension and nervousness in your life. Your emotions are more stable at this time. This could be an excellent time to start a new business in which you could express your creative ideas and artistic talents. You may become very interested in studying music for a hobby. You also could become interested in drama and acting.
OPPOSITION	Do not start any new speculative projects that require new investments. You may lose if you do. The tensions and nervousness will interfere with your judgment so much that you will have a hard time making any decisions. There will be much confusion in your mental and emotional life. Those in authority may appear to be deceiving you at this time.. Their deceit could be a fact or it could be your imagination.

SUN TO PLUTO

CONJUNCT	You will find that you are extremely aggressive and independent at this time. Your leadership and creative abilities are very evident. This aspect improves your vitality tremendously. There may be many important changes in your life which are for the better.
SEXTILE	You will probably become interested in the welfare of your friends. You may become interested in clubs, societies or organizations and you may wish to join one.
SQUARE	Other people's plans and yours may be opposing. Don't force your opinions or plans on others. Compromise once in a while and you will have less trouble. Your independence and aggression may offend those around you causing them to reject you or plot against you. Your nervous tension may undermine your health at this time. This aspect could cause you to get fired from your job or cause a loss in your business.
TRINE	You seem to possess a tremendous vitality now. It may appear that you could do anything you want to do regarding physical activity. This would be a good time to form a partnership with a person you trust and admire. Don't over extend your physical strength and don't over spend.
OPPOSITION	Many opportunities may come your way but make sure they are practical before you take advantage of any of them. You may meet many people who are aggressive and adventurous now. You may be inclined to be more adventurous yourself. You may want to rebel against those in authority to bring about changes or just because you feel like rebelling. Don't do it; the results will be negative.

TRANSIT VENUS

KEYWORDS FOR VENUS

POSITIVE	NEGATIVE
ACTORS AND ACTRESSES	OVER INDULGENCES
ADMIRATION	UNPOPULAR
AFFECTION AND BEAUTY	LAZY
ARTISTIC ENDEAVORS	RUDE
ROMANCES	UGLY
POPULARITY	UPSET EMOTIONS AND DISAPPOINTMENTS
COURTESY	LOSS OF MONEY
ALLURE	BROKEN PROMISES
ATTRACTIVENESS	UNFAITHFUL
EMOTIONS	SELFISHNESS
SOCIAL AFFAIRS	TROUBLE WITH FEMALES RELATIVES AND YOUNG WOMEN
LUXURIES	BROKEN PROMISES
ATTACHMENTS OF ALL KINDS	DOMESTIC UPSETS
MONEY	FEELINGS ARE VERY EASILY HURT
HAPPINESS	SLOPPY
CATS	CARELESS
CHECK BOOKS	
CHILDREN	
CLOTHES	
COMPROMISES	
DANCING	
DIPLOMACY	
ENGAGEMENTS	
FAITHFULNESS	
FAVORS	
FEMALE RELATIVES	
SWEETHEARTS	
GIFTS	

TRANSIT VENUS IN THE HOUSES

HOUSES

1. This will be a very optimistic and cheerful period for you. You usually are very pleasant and tactful at this time. You can express your love and affection for people with ease now. You may have a tendency to view the world through rose tinted glasses.

2. There should be some kind of small financial gains indicated at this time. You may find that you want to spend too lavishly on a new wardrobe. You may receive some type of gift or bonus from the company for which you work. You may gain through women or the public. You may find your sweet tooth is very active at this time and it may affect your health in an adverse way.

3. You will be on friendly terms with your family and relatives. You are more relaxed and peaceful now. May take short pleasure trips. You could receive some sort of message or communication that will please you. You may feel very poetic and very optimistic at this time.

4. This would be an excellent time to repaint the home and redecorate. It is a good time to give parties or plan social affairs in the home. This would be an excellent time to buy a new home or sell the present home for gain. Your interest now is usually centered on the home and the family.

5. You may become involved in a new love affair or become very romantic. Children's recreation and fun may interest you very much at this time. This could be an excellent time to speculate or gamble. Parties, parties, and more parties may be all you're thinking about. This could be a good time to express some of your creative thoughts through poetry.

6. You could become very creative at work and may find that your relationships with your co-workers and associates are excellent. This may be a period where you might be entirely in love with your work. You may over-indulge in rich foods and sweets, causing you serious health problems.

7. You could benefit now through marriage or by forming some business partnership. This would be an excellent time to entertain a friend or partner.

8. This period could cause you to become very interested in financial security. Your partner may receive some financial gain. This would be an excellent time to start a savings account. An insurance policy obtained at this time would be a good investment; you could profit from it greatly at a later date. You may receive a refund check from the government for over-payment of income taxes.

9.   You -may become interested in some form of art or music. The reading of interesting books could give you pleasure now. You may decide at this time to take a long distance trip for pleasure. You may receive some sort of communication from a sister who lives a long distance from you. It is an excellent time for writers to submit a book to their publisher.

10.   Your social contacts made at this time will be very beneficial for you at a later date. You wull be able to communicate with your superiors or bosses. You could make social contacts now that could help you now because everyone seems to be very receptive to you and your ideas.

11.   You could be accepted into a club, society or an organization that you have applied to for membership. You could come in contact with many progressive and artistic people at social functions. Your superiors will give you the honors and credit due you. This could indicate an increase in your income from your profession or business.

12.   You may become very interested in volunteering to work in an institution or with those less fortunate than yourself. You may discover at this time that you have a secret admirer. Or you could become involved in a secret love affair. You may be perfectly content to spend most of your time by yourself. This position may help you to overcome some of your secret enemies.

TRANSIT VENUS ASPECTS

VENUS TO MOON

CONJUNCT

This would be an excellent time to visit those confined to their home or in a hospital. Your home life is very enjoyable now. This would be a good time to entertain in the home. Women seem to be very in tune with you and you will enjoy their company much more than usual. May have many pleasant visits in the home with close friends.

SEXTILE

This is a very favorable time for all love affairs, social gatherings or parties. An excellent time to buy new clothes you have been wanting for some time. Your income will improve. You probably will have many enjoyable visits with relatives and neighbors.

SQUARE

There may be additional expense in the home that will deplete your budget, and you may have many disagreements. with the wife about these additional expenses. Your relationship with your mother may be strained at this time. Social affairs and parties could be boring at this time in your life. Most females will tend to irritate you with their gossip and chit chat. Your health may suffer because of the tension and emotional upset going on in your life.

TRINE

This is an excellent time to plan parties or social affairs. You may over-indulge in rich foods or alcoholic beverages, causing an upset stomach or worse. Your emotions are more stable at this time.

OPPOSITION

This is a bad time to plan parties or to attend any social functions. There may be financial losses because of over spending on recreational or social affairs. Make sure that you don't repeat any gossip you may hear at this time. Don't rely on promises made to you by others.

VENUS TO MERCURY

CONJUNCT

You probably will enjoy taking short trips to visit friends. This would be an excellent time to catch up on all correspondence. A good time to buy and sell by mail.

SEXTILE

You will probably enjoy your vacation more by taking a short trip now. This is an excellent time to communicate with younger people, especially with young women. This aspect could bring about a small financial gain ,or your business may prosper during this period.

SQUARE

Don't break any promises unless you're sure you can keep them. Your social affairs may be very disappointing to you. Refrain from repeating gossip or making harsh statements about others. You could have a tendency to become very selfish during this period.

TRINE   You may enjoy a short trip to a social function. Conditions
                 at work are more pleasurable. You may receive some form
                 of correspondence that will give you great pleasure. You
                 find now that you communicate with younger people much
                 easier.

OPPOSITION   Don't become involved in any public speaking now. Don't
                 write anything in letters that you may regret later. Your
                 love affair or romance may be blocked now; don't force
                 any decisions regarding it during this aspect. Wait till a later
                 day to make any decisions concerning your love affairs be-
                 cause these difficulties will pass with time. The social af-
                 fairs you attend now will probably turn out to be bummers.

VENUS TO VENUS

CONJUNCT   Social affairs and romances become very important to you
                 at this time. A young woman may come into your life who
                 will become very important to you. Social functions will
                 be enjoyable at the present time.

SEXTILE   This would be an excellent time to settle all old disputes in
                 your personal life. A good time to start some small project
                 that would enable you to make an increase in your income.
                 A good time to buy jewelry and cosmetics.

SQUARE   No matter how hard you try to make social functions and
                 your domestic life enjoyable, there is always someone caus-
                 ing friction among the people around you. Don't try to
                 settle disputes between brothers and sisters, they will blame
                 you for interfering. There may be many little disturbing
                 things happening with your co-workers or associates that
                 you will get blamed for. Nothing really serious happens but
                 all the little things will make this a very frustrating time for
                 you.

TRINE   Home and social life are very satisfying now. This is a very
                 lucky time for you. An excellent time to settle old dis-
                 putes with brothers and sisters. Love affairs seem very im-
                 portant to you now. Your income may increase.

OPPOSITION   It doesn't matter what you attempt to do at this time,
                 everyone will seem to be opposing you. Don't get involved
                 in any new love affair because it would only be temporary.
                 Don't start a business or new project with the idea of gain-
                 ing financially because your emotions will affect your judg-
                 ment which will surely be faulty at the present time.

VENUS TO SUN

CONJUNCT
This aspect could cause a very active social life and you could become involved in a new love affair. You could become very interested in helping some member of your family. There could be an increase in your income or business at this time.

SEXTILE
A male friend could be instrumental in presenting you to a social group that you have been trying to get involved with for a long time. There seems to be more group involvement than usual.

SQUARE
There will be many little disturbing things that will make your life miserable. Any new business started at this time could fail or cause a serious financial loss. You may have trouble with younger women at work or in business or with young people.

TRINE
This would be an excellent time for you to take your vacation. Any contact you may have with others at this time should be very enjoyable. You may receive a small gift or a small increase in your income.

OPPOSITION
Your love affairs may suffer because of interference from friends. A woman may cause you some kind of financial loss. Your superiors or boss may say things to you that will hurt your feelings.

VENUS TO MARS

CONJUNCT
You may become very involved in a new love affair or romance. You could be very extravagant at this time and spend too much on luxuries or social affairs. There could be a slight improvement in your income and business.

SEXTILE
You may have the opportunity to settle old problems that have been plaguing you for some time. You may want to take a short vacation or attend an important social affair.

SQUARE
Your budget may suffer at this time because you will have a tendency to spend too much money on luxuries or go to expensive social functions. Your feelings may be hurt because you may think the woman in your life doesn't appreciate you.

TRINE
You may appear very magnetic to the opposite sex. You may gain financially enough to be able to clear up small bills that have been plaguing you for some time. This would be an excellent time to start a new business or project for financial gain.

OPPOSITION
You could be imposed on at this time because of your good nature. Young people could be inconsiderate at this time and this could hurt your feelings. You could have misunderstandings with young women also.

VENUS TO JUPITER

CONJUNCT
VERY LUCKY PERIOD. You may become very popular with the opposite sex. Don't let all this attention go to your head. You should have much success in your finances and business.

SEXTILE
Don't become too extravagant and over spend on luxuries and good times. May receive a citation or compliment from those in authority or the boss. This is an excellent time to stabilize your love life or your position in your social crowd.

SQUARE
Your feelings may be super sensitive at this time. You could be hurt by the slightest negative remark from those around you. Your friends may not appreciate you the way you think they should. You could hurt them or not appreciate them in the same way. You may have a reduction in your income or business profits may not be what they should be.

TRINE
This would be an excellent time to expand your business. Your income should increase substantially at this time. LUCK! Some friend may do you a favor because of past favors you did for him. Your domestic and social affairs are really enjoyable at this time. You may be over optimistic. Watch it because this aspect only lasts a couple of days.

OPPOSITION
This could cause a possible loss in finances or the business. Your judgement may be faulty at this time because emotions are so easily upset. Don't get involved in any "get rich" schemes. This would be a poor time to start any sort of new investments. Young women may give you a bad time.

VENUS TO SATURN

CONJUNCT
You may have a romance with an older person or you may form a friendship with an older person. This would be an excellent time to make a budget and stick to it.

SEXTILE
You could travel a long distance for a job. May make many older friends on the new job. This move now usually indicates a promotion or gain in income.

SQUARE
This is a very frustrating time. Your feelings will be hurt by the slightest thing. You will be super touchy about everything. Your romance and your friendships with others seems to suffer. No one seems to appreciate what a great person you are. There may be loss in income or financial losses in business caused by misjudgement. This faulty judgement is caused by your lack of emotional stability at this time.

TRINE   Your love life and social activities are more stable and ser-
             ious. You may receive a recommendation from the boss or
             a friend that will enable you to get a promotion at work.
             Some sort of publicity would help your business to increase.
             A research project would interest you at this time.

OPPOSITION   People may criticize you at this time for no reason at all.
             You may find that some older male is opposing your ideas
             and plans at work. You may have many disagreements and
             disputes with those close to you. You may become very
             depressed at this time because everything and everybody
             appear to be against you.

VENUS TO URANUS

CONJUNCT   Don't reveal any personal secrets or any of your personal
             plans. There could be an unexpected and unusual love
             affair or an unusual friendship is formed with an active and
             progressive type of person. This usually is a good time for
             business or an increase in your income.

SEXTILE   This could be an exciting time for social affairs and
             romances. This would be a good time to start some unusual
             hobby or project. You may become very creative and
             artistic at this time.

SQUARE   You may unexpectedly break off an old love affair or separ-
             ate from an old friend. There may be much turmoil within
             the domestic life. Could be losses in business or reductions
             in income. You could become very extravagant and over
             spend on luxuries and your budget would suffer. Many
             unexpected changes occur in your life and all of them detri-
             mental to you.

TRINE   You may become involved in some unusual and unexpected
             love affairs or may form some unusual friendships at this
             time. This would be an excellent time to start an unusual
             hobby. You may receive an unexpected financial gain
             through a young woman or through young people.

OPPOSITION   Old friendships and your romances may be broken because
             of arguments or quarrelling. You may become too defensive
             at this time because your feelings are too easily hurt. Your
             family or relatives may be prying into your life or inter-
             fering with your activities, causing you to become very
             upset.

VENUS TO NEPTUNE

CONJUNCT   You could have many pleasant trips, picnics or social events under this aspect. Your creative and artistic talents may come to the front at this time. You could possibly become interested in studying music for a hobby.

SEXTILE   Any trips taken at this time could be very profitable and pleasant. Your long waited for desires and wishes may be fulfilled now. A trip may be taken with relatives or friends to a sea resort.

SQUARE   There may be some confusion on your job; you may not know how long it is going to last. A young woman or some young person may deliberately deceive you. There may be much gossip about you or you may become involved in a scandal.

TRINE   People may make many promises to you at this time but they won't keep them. Your desires and wishes are more realistic and there is a better chance that you may be able to obtain them. This would be an excellent time to re-decorate (the furniture and the home).

OPPOSITION   Your judgement is faulty because you may let your imagination run away with your common sense. You may cause financial losses by being over extravagant at this time. You could possibly spend too much money on social functions or too much on luxuries. There could be a younger girl or woman who is deceiving you about something. Your feelings are super sensitive at the present time and cause you trouble with those close to you.

VENUS TO PLUTO

CONJUNCT   You may have an unconscious desire for new love affairs and social events, but you won't admit it. This would be an excellent time to complete all pending projects and to start new ones. You may have a tendency at this time to want to pry into the affairs of others; if you do, it could cause you much difficulty.

SEXTILE   You may make friends with younger people or become involved with a younger woman. You are unusually satisfied with your social life. This would be an excellent time to increase your income or improve your business.

SQUARE   This aspect could cause you to break off a romance because you may be trying to force your will on the loved one. You may have a tendency to judge too harshly and to demand too much from others. There may be financial losses at this time because your emotions interfere with your judgement. You may make a fool of yourself with your relatives.

TRINE	The key word here is "LUCK". The sky may appear to be the limit. Don't push it too far because this aspect doesn't last very long. There will be substantial financial gains in relation to your income or business. You may enjoy many social events with your friends and loved ones.
OPPOSITION	You may become involved in a sudden and passionate love affair but it won't last long. The end result of the love affair may cause you to become very depressed. You may come in contact with a lot of aggressive and rebellious people who could upset you a great deal. Your feelings could be hurt by the slightest thing. You could also become very creative and artistic at this time.

TRANSIT MERCURY

KEYWORDS FOR MERCURY

POSITIVE	NEGATIVE
WRITING OR CORRESPONDENCE	BAD NEWS
STUDY	POOR CONCENTRATION
MAKE SPEECHES	IMPULSIVE SPEAKING
SALES OR COMMISSIONS	LOSS OF SALES OR COMMISSIONS
MINOR OFFICIALS	TROUBLE WITH MINOR OFFICIALS
MESSENGERS OR LETTERS	TROUBLE WHILE ON TRIPS
ADVERTISERS	LATE FOR APPOINTMENTS
PUBLISHERS	GOSSIP OR LIES
BOOKS AND STATIONERY CONCERNS	LOSS IN SMALL BUSINESS DEALS
TEACHERS	PETTY WORRIES
STUDENTS	INTENSE MENTAL ACTIVITY
LAWYERS	MISUNDERSTANDINGS
YOUNG PEOPLE OR YOUNG MEN	SARCASTIC SPEECH
SHORT TRIPS	TROUBLE WITH YOUNG PEOPLE OR YOUNG MEN
DEALERS	
SPEED	
READING	
TRANSPORTATION	
EDUCATION	
CONTRACTS	
LEARNS EASILY	

TRANSIT MERCURY IN THE HOUSES

HOUSES

1. Your thoughts may turn to self improvement programs and how to create a more attractive public image of yourself. You become very interested in new ideas and the changes these ideas bring about are very important to you. You may try your hand at writing or become very interested in reading literature. Watch your speech at this time because you may have a tendency to make rash statements. Small and irritating things could upset you very much.

2. You may be able to improve your finances by taking a short trip at this time. Be more sympathetic and courteous with associates and friends. Hasty speech and rash statements or promises could cost you money.

3. Your mind will be more on traveling at this time. You may receive some sort of communication from relatives. The urge to write is very strong at this time. You may be inclined to sign a contract. Your mind could become very restless and over-active. It would be a poor time for you to take any classes because your concentration is very poor.

4. You may become very involved in plans relating to the home. One of the parents may communicate with you now. This would be an excellent time to sign contracts regarding the home or real estate. A relative may come for a short visit. This could bring about changes in your profession or business.

5. You may become very interested in a new hobby. You may have the urge to speculate, invest, gamble or go to the horse races. You may try to make up your mind which of your friends are reliable and dependable. May become very interested in young children's educational programs. May become very interested in communicating with those you love.

6. May be over concerned about your work or may become bored with the job and start looking for a new one. This would be an excellent time to check your diet or make an appointment with the doctor for a physical check up. You may start looking for another apartment because you want to find one that will allow you to keep a small pet.

7. This is the time to sign any contracts you may have pending. You may decide at this time to go into business for yourself. A visit to the doctor or the dentist is possible at this time. You may give an impromptu speech at some public function. May take a short trip to visit with a close friend.

8. This would be an excellent time to help the partner with his financial problems. Check all of your insurance policies to see if they cover you sufficiently. Take care of all tax problems at this time. Some may experiment with sex and drugs. Some may receive communication regarding a legacy or inheritance.

9. You may receive a letter or phone call from those living a long distance away. You may start making plans for the next vacation. Authors and writers may be waiting to receive word from their publishers. You may become involved with legal documents, a lawyer or a judge.

10. Your ideas and plans may be all directed towards profession or business. This is an excellent time to buy with the idea of a quick turn over for profit. You may sign some contracts that have to do with profession or business.

11. You may become involved with the type of friends who are interested in improving their intellectual abilities. A club or society may give you an award for an outstanding thing you have done. This could be an excellent time to help the younger people. There may be a slight improvement in your income or you may receive a slight promotion on the job.

12. This would be an excellent time to get involved in a research project. You may visit a library to find information for this project. You could possibly visit a young friend in the hospital. Avoid excessive daydreaming. Be very realistic and practical in all of your financial plans. Think and plan for the future.

TRANSIT MERCURY ASPECTS

MERCURY TO MOON

CONJUNCT

This aspect tends to bring about short distance trips. You may become very involved in answering correspondence or phoning people. There may be little minor changes in the home. You could receive a communication from your relatives.

SEXTILE

You may receive pleasant news that will make you happy. This is an excellent time to write letters, attend lectures or classes. Check all information received at this time to make sure it is correct.

SQUARE

You may be so emotionally upset that it will interfere with your thinking and judgement. There may be much tension and nervousness at this time. Bad news has a tendency to upset you. You may have trouble at this time remembering things you should. This aspect doesn't last long so take it easy. This could bring many little irritating things and confusion on a trip.

TRINE

This is an excellent time to make minor changes in the home. You will probably have a pleasant time on all short trips taken now. It's a good time to start a new class. You find that you will be able to communicate with those around you with ease. Excellent time to catch up on all correspondence and to make phone calls.

OPPOSITION

Make sure you explain everything very carefully at this time because people have a tendency to misunderstand you. There could be many little misunderstandings with women and the public. Don't push anything at this time. This aspect won't last long. Your judgement may be faulty now because your emotions may interfere with your thinking clearly. Postpone any decisions till a later date.

MERCURY TO MERCURY

CONJUNCT

This is a very stimulating aspect for the mental processes. You will be able to talk and communicate, very fluently. You may have many inspirational ideas at the present time but don't over do it. Don't make any rash statements that you could be sorry about later.

SEXTILE

This would be an excellent time to take short trips with the youngsters. Plans that you and your relatives have been making may materialize now. This aspect is very good time for speeches or any form of teaching or lecturing.

SQUARE	There are many little irritating things going on in your life. There could be much confusion and misunderstanding with any type of communication. Make sure that you explain everything very thoroughly. Don't let yourself be provoked into any kind of arguments. Don't make any impulsive decisions at the present. Wait!
TRINE	This would be an excellent time to take care of all correspondence. Excellent time to communicate with relatives. You could have many pleasant social events with younger people. A good time to take a short trip for pleasure or business.
OPPOSITION	There is much tension and nervousness. You may have trouble sleeping at this time because you can't turn your thinking off. You could possibly lose your job because of arguments with co-workers. Your health may suffer due to too much tension. Don't make any rash statements that you may be sorry for later.

MERCURY TO VENUS

CONJUNCT	You may receive many invitations and may attend many social affairs now. You appear to write and speak more fluently at this time. You may take a very enjoyable trip with younger woman or younger people. You may receive some important piece of correspondence from a young woman or friend.
SEXTILE	You will show good judgement at this time in buying luxury items. You will find communicating with friends and younger people very enjoyable. You may take a short trip for pleasure or business.
SQUARE	You may receive a communication that will upset you temporarily; it will probably be nothing too serious. There may be many little irritating things happening that could disturb your peace of mind. This aspect could be favorable for communicating with those in authority.
TRINE	Short trips taken with relatives or friends could be very enjoyable. You may receive letters, phone calls or correspondence from friends, relatives, or a young woman that would please you very much.
OPPOSITION	You may become involved with many young people on a trip that you had to take unexpectedly. You may receive unexpected invitations to a social function. Some young woman may be trying to interfere with one or more of your plans.

MERCURY TO SUN

CONJUNCT — This is an excellent aspect for any type of business transactions. This is a good time to look for a new job. An excellent time for teaching or any literary work or efforts. You may take a trip for business reasons.

SEXTILE — Salesmen under this aspect can present and persuade the customer to buy. You will be able to express your view point or opinion without any adverse results. It is a good time for any public speaking you may wish to do. Also, would be a good time to sign any contracts or deeds.

SQUARE — This is a bad time for business or any legal matters. This is a poor time to take any kind of trip. Those in authority may be opposing your ideas or plans. Wait until later to push any plans or ideas. Your nervousness and tension could cause accidents.

TRINE — Your ideas and plans cna be presented without any misunderstanding and those in authority are more receptive at this time. An excellent time to start a new project. You may increase your income or improve your business. Excellent time to sign all contracts and legal documents.

OPPOSITION — You may receive some form of communication that could give you the feeling everyone is opposing your plans and ideas. This could create much tension and nervousness in your life. There will be many minor irritations while on a trip.

MERCURY TO MARS

CONJUNCT — Your judgement may be faulty at this time because you are so impulsive. Watch what you say or do and especially be careful in what you write. Read all fine print in any contracts which you might sign at this time.

SEXTILE — Your judgement is good at this time because you are very mentally alert. Your speech will quite possibly be more humorous and pleasant now. You may take a very enjoyable trip at this time.

SQUARE	You may be very impulsive in your speech and actions. You may be under so much tension that your impulsive speech may offend those around you and cause many disputes or arguments. This definitely is not the time to do any buying or selling. Your judgement is faulty due to impatience and the desire to get things moving, no matter if it is right or wrong.
TRINE	Your judgement is much better but watch that impulsiveness. This would be an excellent time to start any new project that needs physical strength. Excellent period for buying or selling. A good time to take a trip.
OPPOSITION	You may have a tendency to be too aggressive or quarrelsome. Take it easy and listen to other people's ideas and opinions. The tension and nervousness could cause you to have many muscle spasms. Don't blurt out anything that may offend others. This is an accident aspect and you may also have trouble with your car.

MERCURY TO JUPITER

CONJUNCT	You may receive recognition or get an award for your past deeds or past work record. This is an excellent time to handle all legal matters. You are more tolerant and understanding in regards to other's opinions. Excellent time to take a trip for business reasons. Your income may increase or your business may improve.
SEXTILE	Your judgement is better because your thinking is clearer and calmer. This is an excellent time to catch up on all correspondence. You may become involved with an old friend you haven't seen in years.
SQUARE	Your judgement is bad because of nervousness and impulsiveness. There may be minor losses in business because of poor judgement. Your thinking is too optimistic at this time. Don't make any important decisions or sign any contracts or legal documents. If there is a lawsuit pending, it may be decided against you. There may be many delays and disappointments in any appointments you may have at this time.
TRINE	This is a lucky period, but it's a short one. Your income may improve and you may receive pleasant news regarding your finances. Your judgement and timing are excellent at this time. Excellent time to take a short trip for business or pleasure or to visit with relatives.
OPPOSITION	Your in-laws or close relatives seem to be opposing all of your ideas or plans. You may misjudge your physical strength at this time and overwork, which may endanger your health. You could become extremely tense and nervous. Relax and take it easy.

MERCURY TO SATURN

CONJUNCT   This aspect could cause anxiety and depressions. You will become more serious and will pay more attention to details. Your speech will become more eloquent and precise. You may become more interested in facts, not opinions.

SEXTILE   A period of time when you will become more interested in small details. This is an excellent time to make long-range plans for the future.

SQUARE   You will find that your depressions and anxieties will be hard to overcome. Put off answering all correspondences that you can. This will be bad for your finances or for business. It seems impossible to be able to communicate with older people. There will be many minor irritations on any trip you may take at this time.

TRINE   Your thinking will be very serious and you won't be interested in any superficial things. Excellent time to sign any contracts that will take a long time to mature. You seem to enjoy the company of older people more at this time. You may visit one of your older relatives. Your dad seems to be able to communicate easier now.

OPPOSITION   If you take any trips for business, you'll suffer a loss or won't be able to make your appointments. A very poor time for finances. Put off signing any contracts you can because any contract signed at this time would be a detriment instead of bringing about a profit. May find that your correspondence is a pain in the neck or you might not receive letters that you are waiting for. This is a very poor time to start a new job or any new project.

MERCURY TO URANUS

CONJUNCT   This aspect will increase your mental activity and you'll find that your intuition is more reliable. This will be a very active time for those who write or those who invent. You may decide unexpectedly to take a short business trip. You will find that your mental processes work at lightening speed and are very accurate.

SEXTILE   You may become super independent at this time. You will have enjoyable times with your progressive and active friends. You will have many creative ideas and this would be an excellent time to start new projects.

SQUARE   You may stew and fret about every little thing. You may become too aggressive and have arguments with friends, relatives or neighbors. You will be very nervous and tense. Don't make any decisions at this time because you're too impulsive and will jump to conclusions without all the facts. Your business may suffer under this aspect; don't sign any new contracts without reading the fine print.

TRINE	You may take enjoyable short trips with younger and more active friends. You may find that you are becoming interested in the occult, metaphysical or philosophical studies. This is an excellent time to start any new and progressive projects. Your business will be improved under this aspect.
OPPOSITION	You may become over aggressive and this could cause arguments and disputes with friends and relatives. Your business may suffer under this aspect. Tension and nervousness could affect your health in an adverse way. You may have trouble sleeping at this time or have trouble turning off your thoughts.

MERCURY TO NEPTUNE

CONJUNCT	You could become very intuitive at this time. Pay attention to your hunches. You may be able to express your thoughts in inspirational writing or in a poetic way. You may have confused thinking or some distorted ideas and plans.
SEXTILE	This could help you to express yourself in a poetic way. People will listen to you more and be more receptive to your ideas and plans. This is not a very physical aspect. It will work more on your emotions and thinking.
SQUARE	Don't get involved in any kind of gossip. Control your tongue. Think twice before you say anything. Your judgement may be very bad because of your lack of practical ideas and thoughts. Be honest in everything you do or say. Your income or business could suffer. Be careful about signing any contracts at this time. You may have trouble receiving your mail or you may receive confusing messages from someone.
TRINE	This is an inspirational aspect for anyone involved in art, music, literature, acting or photography. You may receive important news from someone who lives a good distance from you. Your imagination is very active and creative at this time. You may try your hand at poetic writing or in writing a short story.
OPPOSITION	At this time there may be much mental confusion and confused ideas and plans. You could have a hard time trying to make up your mind about something. Your concentration is bad; every little thing will have a tendency to distract you from what you were thinking about. You may receive garbled and confusing messages. You may hear gossip or scandalous news that may shock you. This is a bad time to sign any contracts. May lose in business.

MERCURY TO PLUTO

CONJUNCT   Your income or business may improve considerably. You may receive shocking news about young people. You may be asked to give a public speech at this time.

SEXTILE   This is a good time to compelte that project you haven't finished. Your judgement is excellent at the present time. You could become very subtle and tactful in your manner of speaking.

SQUARE   This aspect could create a lot of tension and nervousness which could affect your health in an adverse way. Keep calm and relax more. You may be inclined now to gossip and be deceitful. Check all your bills to see if the billing is correct. You may have trouble communicating at this time because everything comes out differently than you intended. Make sure that you are correct and concise to prevent confusion in communications. Don't over spend on pleasure trips or your budget may suffer. You may have trouble with your car.

TRINE   Publicity would be very good for business now. This should bring about a favorable increase in your finances. You could be accepted into a club or society or organization which you have been trying to join for sometime. You may help some younger person realize his ambition or goal. You are able to communicate with the public in a special way, such as making a public speech which endorses an organization.

OPPOSITION   You could be separated form an old friend because you are too outspoken or impulsive. You may find others opposing you because of something you may have said. There may be many arguments with younger brothers and sisters. Your mail may be mislaid or be sent to another address because of a mistake made by the post office.

TRANSITS OF NEW MOON

NEW MOON IN THE HOUSES

HOUSES

1. You may be active physically. Relax more and stay calm. Put off today' what you can do tomorrow because too much activity may affect your strength and health.

2. There may be many fluctuations in your financial program. You may lose financially by over spending or by being careless.

3. Your thinking may be over active. This could cause you many headaches. This is a good time to handle all correspondence and paper work. You may take short trips or may receive some form of communication from relatives or neighbors.

4. Changes in the home; you may have many visitors in the home. This would be an excellent time to entertain the family in the home. There may be a slight beneficial or adverse changes in the profession of business.

5. This position could stimulate love affairs or romances. You probably will become more interested in the affairs of children. You may wish to invest, speculate or gamble. You may wish to spend more time working on your hobby.

6. You may have a slight improvement in your occupation or on your job. Your health may be better at this time. May decide to change your diet or style of dress. There may be a change in your weight.

7. You may experience changes in regard to a partner or you may make some changes in contracts. This position could improve cooperation with a partner or close friend. There could be a lawsuit pending.

8. This is an excellent time to help a partner with financial problems. Don't over spend or invest in any new projects. Watch your health. May have trouble sleeping at this time.

9. You may become involved in an argument with the in-laws. Don't take any long trips because they could be very costly during this period.

10. The changes going on within your profession or business may give you some concern about finances. Be careful not to criticize your superior or boss.

11. May have many arguments and quarrels with friends now. A project or program that you are trying to complete now will not be completed. You may be thinking about putting new plans into effect, don't, wait until a later time to do this.

·12. If you have any plans in the making at this time, don't reveal them until a later date. You may feel very restricted or held back because of circumstances or people in your life. Play it cool, this will blow over. Everything may seem to be going too slow for you now; don't let these circumstances cause you to lose your temper.

NEW MOON CONJUNCTION
THE NATAL PLANETS

PLANETS

SUN

This could bring about changes in your life regarding health, males, females and domestic affairs. The force of this conjunction could be the cause of a turning point in your life.

MOON

You may suddenly change your mind about certain things. in your personal and home life. This placement also could cause many ups and downs with the public, home life and those who are close to you.

MERCURY

Your mind is over active at this time. You may receive an important communication. You may be thinking about taking a short trip for pleasure or business or you may actually take such a trip. If there are any adverse aspects at this time, you may criticize others too much or they may criticize you very harshly.

VENUS

This aspect could increase your popularity and bring about a new love affair or romance. You could spend money on new clothes to make yourself feel more attractive.

MARS

You may become very impulsive, energetic and daring at this time. May be many quarrels and disagreements with others. Be very cautious in everything you do or say.

JUPITER

You may become over expansive and generous at this time. Your outlook will be very optimistic. This is a lucky time in all areas of your life. This would be an excellent time to start any new project that you may have been planning for a long time.

SATURN

It may appear to you that everything has come to a complete halt. Don't try to start any new projects at this time. You may become very serious and thoughtful or you could become very depressed and pessimistic. Depressed moods may affect your health in an adverse way. Watch it!

URANUS

This could bring many unexpected changes in all areas of your life. You may find yourself breaking away from old ways of doing things or breaking away from old ties in your life. There may be many new people coming into your life. Use the utmost caution if you begin any new project at this time.

NEPTUNE

Your feelings are certain to be over stimulated under this aspect. Be very realistic and practical in everything you do. Think twice or three times before you make any decisions. Your feelings and emotions may cause you to make mistakes.

PLUTO

You may find that you are more aggressive and independent at this time. Any changes that are brought about usually are permanent.

TRANSITS OF FULL MOON

FULL MOON IN THE HOUSES

HOUSES

1. This would be an excellent time to start any new projects. You will probably become very interested in or involved in personal and business affairs. Relax and don't get in such a hurry and you may prevent accidents in the home or public. Some may feel tense and restless and others may feel very lethargic. This will depend on the aspects.

2. This could indicate gains or losses. It would depend on the aspects the full moon makes. Be conservative in all of your spending.

3. You may receive some form of communication from brothers, sisters, or relatives. You may take a trip to visit a relative or old neighbor. This is an excellent time to catch up on all over due correspondence.

4. This would be an excellent time to investigate a real estate investment or to buy a home. There should be some kind of changes going on within the home or in domestic affairs. You may become concerned about one of the parents. There may be a slight change in the business.

5. You may take more interest in the affairs of children, either yours or someone elses. You may become very interested in speculation or gambling. You may be thinking about a vacation. Don't overdo in having fun.

6. This would be an excellent time to help a co-worker. Watch your health very closely; if you have any problems check with your doctor as soon as possible. Excellent time to improve any skills needed at work.

7. The keyword here is "CO-OPERATION". Make an extra effort to get along with partner, wife or husband. This is a good time to deal with the public. May be a good time to visit a close friend.

8. Help the partner to improve his financial program. Check all insurance policies to make sure they cover you sufficiently. Take care of all tax problems. Watch your health.

9. You may become interested in the welfare of your in-laws. A good time to take up the study of philosophy or religion. You may become interested in attending church regularly. Best time to check all legal documents.

10. This would be an excellent time to put forth more effort to improve your business or professional goals. Don't get carried away with your ambition as this might cause trouble in your domestic life.

11. Very good time to improve your relationship with friends and groups. You may obtain some of your most cherished desires and hopes. Co-operation is important at this time. You may be able to improve your income through your profession or business.

12. Make plans but don't reveal them until a later date. You may want to go into seclusion now. Be practical in everything you do in relation to business or finances.

TRANSITS OF NORTH NODE

TRANSIT NORTH NODE

CONJUNCT

Allow an orb of two (2) degrees approaching the conjunction.

PLANET

SUN

Your superiors may give you credit for something that they think you have done, but it will be someone else's work for which you get the credit. Usually with this aspect you receive many invitations to social affairs. Your friends will show their appreciation of you by word or actions.

MOON

You will assume more responsibility cheerfully and will be rewarded for this attitude by an increase in your income.

MERCURY

This will be a very active period for you. Anything occuring at this time usually is of a temporary nature.

VENUS

Your love affairs or romances may occupy your time to a greater extent at this time. There may be a slight increase in income.

MARS

You may become over optimistic now. Be practical in everything you do or say. If you have to make a decision now, be very cautious.

JUPITER

You may have a tendency to see everything through rose tinted glasses. The desire to succeed is very strong.

SATURN

This is an excellent time to make long range plans. Your ambitions are usually more practical and realistic at this time.

URANUS

This is an excellent time to work extra hard toward your business goals. Luck comes to you in the form of opportunities to improve your business or profession.

NEPTUNE

Do not act on intuitive ideas or hunches. Think twice before you decide on anything because your judgement may be faulty.

PLUTO

Make sure that you pay strict attention to all details and facts. Use all of your knowledge and past experience to handle any unexpected problems.

TRANSITS OF SOUTH NODE

CONJUNCT

PLANETS

SUN You may make a decision to sell some property to pay your overdue bills. You may withdraw from your savings account to pay bills.

MOON Don't let your enthusiasm or impulsiveness let you make a decision without all the facts. Be very practical in everything you do or say.

MERCURY Don't let tension or nervousness cause you to lose your temper. You may become very pessimistic. Try to keep relaxed and calm at all times.

VENUS Your love life, romance or social life may be very disappointing to you at this time. Don't spend too much money on recreation or luxuries, such as clothing, jewelry or other unneeded items.

MARS You may find it will be hard to borrow money or your income may suffer. Slow down and use caution in your driving. Be extra careful around old buildings at this time.

JUPITER Things may appear to be going too slow and you may try to speed them up. Take it easy and relax; you can't force anything at this time. There may be problems concerning the home or your business now.

SATURN· Don't sign any contract without reading the fine print. Any secret that you may be trying to keep from the public may come out in the open at this time.

URANUS There may be many unexpected delays in regards to your hopes and desires. Refrain from being impulsive. Any decisions made now without careful consideration may be faulty.

NEPTUNE Some unexpected events may bring new people into your life. These people may try to persuade you to make a decision that you would prefer to make later.

PLUTO You may become very aggressive and quarrelsome at this time and try to force your opinions on others. Compromise and cooperate with others to prevent further friction and trouble.

TRANSITS OF MOON

TRANSITS OF MOON

KEYWORDS FOR MOON

POSITIVE	NEGATIVE
EMOTIONS-HAPPINESS	IRRITABILITY
WOMEN (MATURE) (HEALTH)	ILL HEALTH
PUBLIC FUNCTIONS	DAYDREAMING
SYMPATHY	UNPOPULAR
MATERNAL AFFECTIONS	DISAPPOINTMENTS
DOMESTIC AFFAIRS	GRIEF OR FEARFULNESS
WIFE	WORRIES
MOTHER	LOSS IN FINANCES AND BUSINESS
CHANGES	
CHILDREN	
HOME	
SILVER MONEY	
FLUIDS	
SMALL IMPROVEMENTS IN FINANCES	

TRANSIT MOON IN THE HOUSES

HOUSES

1.   This is an excellent time to start new projects or businesses. Your mood could change very drastically at this time and cause you much confusion. Avoid all impulsive actions because you could become very careless and have an accident.

2.   This usually indicates many ups and downs in finances. Don't do any impulsive spending. This would be an excellent time to start a savings account. Handle all business promptly that relates to your finances.

3.   This would be an excellent time to catch up on your reading and correspondence. You could start a class that would benefit you now. Short trips may be important for business or to visit relatives.

4.   Your domestic affairs may have many ups and downs. You may enjoy entertaining in the home at this time. This would be an excellent time to start a project or to invest in real estate. Also, a good time to finish any project you have already started.

5.   This would be an excellent time to express some of your creative and artistic ideas or plans. Fun, social affairs and recreational events will appeal to you at this time. You may become involved in a project or program concerning younger people's education.

6.   You may become very interested in improving your relationship and means of communication with co-workers or associates. This would be an excellent time to give an associate a helping hand. You may become very interested in over-hauling your wardrobe or revising your health program. This is a very good time to have a complete physical check up.

7.   You may want to participate in a public affair. This is an excellent time to work with the partner on a joint project. You may enjoy parties and social affairs much more at this time. This could be a good time to see your dentist.

8.   Your sex drive may be strong and you may feel particularly amorous at this time. This could improve your sexual relationship with your marriage partner. This would be an excellent time to study astrology or any occult subject. There could be many changes in regards to your partner's finances. The aspects would determine if there were gains or losses.

9.   Your interest will turn to philosophical and religious subjects. You may be interested in taking a long distance trip and you may actually make a trip at this time. You may dream or remember your dreams more often. You could receive some form of communication from a friend in a foreign country. You may have an appointment with a lawyer or a judge. It's possible you may have to testify in a lawsuit.

10.   This would be an excellent time to make changes in your business. You may feel that you should travel for business reasons. You may feel the need to concentrate on all business contracts or affairs. This could indicate an important change in your domestic affairs.

11.   There may be many changes in your hopes and desires. There could be many ups and downs in regard to income from the business or profession. There may be many changes going on in your friends lives. The results of these changes will depend on the aspects. You could attend a social affair or testimonial a dinner for a friend. This would be a good time to get involved in a fund raising project.

12.   This would be a good time to visit a friend in a hospital or institution. Your sleeping may be very restless and dissatisfying. Your pep or vitality may be at its lowest. Avoid too much daydreaming and be practical in all financial affairs.

TRANSIT MOON ASPECTS

MOON TO MOON

CONJUNCT   You may spend more time in the company of women. You may be very tense and nervous which could cause you health problems. This may indicate many new changes coming up in the next month.

SEXTILE   Your emotions and thinking are working in a more harmonious way. It would be an excellent time for you to catch up on all correspondence that relates to the public. All changes that are going on in your life can be handled easier.

SQUARE   Don't make any impulsive changes in your life without first checking to see if the plans are practical. You may be very tense and nervous and easily upset. There may be many disagreements or arguments with women at this time. Your home life seems to be in constant turmoil. This could affect your health in an adverse way. Watch what you eat because your stomach is easily upset during this aspect.

TRINE   This is an excellent period for anything relating to the public. Any publicity concerning your business or profession could be very beneficial to you. Your relationships with women, wife and mother are very harmonious at this time. The condition of your health is much better now.

OPPOSITION You could be separated from women, wife or mother because of disagreements or arguments. There may be many adverse changes going on in the home or in domestic affairs. It may appear to you that all females are against you.

MOON TO MERCURY

CONJUNCT   You could become very temperamental at this time and your emotions may interfere with your clear thinking and planning ability. You may spend too much money on vacations or some type of recreational activities.

SEXTILE   Your head may be full of progressive ideas and plans. Now would be an excellent time to put them to use. This is a good time to catch up on all old correspondence and to sign any business or professional contracts. This is an excellent time for business or work.

SQUARE   This may be a very frustrating time, with little irritating things interfering with business or profession. Your judgment may be faulty because you will have trouble remembering things, such as appointments or dates with important women. You may become very tense, nervous and have a tendency to gossip at this time. There may be much trouble in any form of communication.

TRINE   This would be an excellent time to catch up on all types of correspondence. Your judgment and memory are very good so it would be a good time to make any important decisions that you have facing you. This is a very good time to sign any contracts or legal documents. You could make short trips for business purposes and gain by the trip. Your communications and relationships with women and the public are very favorable.

OPPOSITION   You may find that you can speak very fluently at this time. Any publicity in regards to business or profession would be very beneficial to you now. You could promise more than you can deliver. Be careful that you don't sign any contracts or legal papers without reading the fine print. This is an excellent time to carry out any routine work.

MOON TO VENUS

CONJUNCT   Your creative and artistic talents are at their height. You will have a strong desire at this time to attend parties or social functions. You will be very charming and lucky. You may spend too much on entertainment and social affairs.

SEXTILE   You can be very pleasant and charming at this time without any special effort. To a male this could indicate a successful marriage. Your social graces are functioning at their utmost. You may find the opposite sex attracted to you also.

SQUARE   You may become very lazy now and your appearance may suffer. You may become very sloppy about your dress. You may have such an intense desire for parties and fun, that other areas, such as work may suffer. You may have arguments and quarrels with the women in the home because too much money is being spent on luxuries or social affairs. You may be inclined to buy very expensive clothes at this time.

TRINE   This aspect will enable you to show your creativeness in the style of your dress. You may receive many compliments on your clothing. You may buy decorations or furniture for the home at a bargain price. You may gain financially in business or profession by dealing with the public or women. This is an excellent time to take a honeymoon.

OPPOSITION   There may be many quarrels or disagreements with your wife because of overspending money on fun or luxuries that you can't afford. This is a very bad time to plan a party or to entertain because of the excessive expense involved. Also, there would be many arguments or strife amongst the guests. You will find that your feelings are easily hurt, the slightest little thing will offend you. Don't be over sensitive and take everything said and done as if it were meant for you.

MOON TO SUN

CONJUNCT   Your vitality is much stronger at this time. It will bring new life into old projects and give you the energy to begin new projects. This aspect may bring about an intense desire to travel. It could make you more popular and your company more in demand by women.

SEXTILE   By accepting new responsibility and gladly accepting more work, you could receive a promotion or increase in business. You will quit worrying about past events and concentrate on the present things. You may gain financially by dealing with the public and women.

SQUARE   You may be very tense and nervous at this time and it could cause you to have a short fuse on your temper. The least little thing may cause you to explode. Don't try to force your own way now. You may have many clashes with authority figures, males or father. You may lose in business or profession during this time. Control yourself!

TRINE   Your relationships with authority figures, males, or father are very harmonious at this time. You may receive a raise or a promotion or your business may increase. Public officials are more receptive to your ideas or plans. The opposite sex may be attracted to you now.

OPPOSITION Old domestic problems may be brought to conclusion now and something may be done about them. This could bring an old project to completion. This is an excellent time to listen to the advice of an expert or a trusted friend. This may bring on arguments or quarrels with males, husband or father.

MOON TO MARS

CONJUNCT   This is a very intense period because of all the excessive physical and emotional activities. These could cause exhaustion and you may become easily irritated. You could become very impulsive or impatient when things appear to be moving too slowly for you.

SEXTILE   This aspect could cause you to be too easily excited and impulsive. Don t let yourself become involved in any self pity.

SQUARE   There is much tension and nervousness involved under this aspect. It could cause you to become very impulsive and cause you to have temper tantrums. There can be many quarrels and arguments, also carelessness and may involve you in an accident. Your stomach could be easily upset during this time. May have many difficulties with females.

TRINE	Your relationships with women and the public are very favorable now. This could indicate a gain in your profession or business. You may be subjected to many changes in your moods. Your domestic changes will be favorable. A good time to invest in real estate for a quick turn over in profit.
OPPOSITION	All women who you come in contact with seem to be opposing you at this time. The public will not be receptive to any of your creative ideas or plans. This is a poor time to have anything to do with any public officials, especially if it is a woman. Too much speed and carelessness could cause an accident. Slow down in your driving and be very cautious.

MOON TO JUPITER

CONJUNCT	You may be over optimistic at this time and may have disappointments. You may be able to relate to those with emotional problems because you're more compassionate and understanding. A public official may help you to gain financially. A good time to get married. You're more carefree and happier than usual under this aspect.
SEXTILE	You may gain financially by dealing with the public and women. A very good time to take care of legal matters or to deal with your publisher. Any publicity relating to your business will be very beneficial to you now.
SQUARE	This is a very poor time to speculate, gamble or try any "get rich" schemes. May have losses in business due to being too optimistic and less practical about everything. You may have a tendency to overeat and this could cause you to gain weight. Promises made to you at this time by others are not kept. This is a poor time to invest in real estate or a home.
TRINE	This is a very LUCKY PERIOD. Your income or your business is sure to improve. This is an excellent time to buy a new home or start a business. Your contract with public officials, lawyers, and judges will be beneficial for you. Any lawsuits pending could be brought to a successful conclusion. Your judgment and timing are excellent now.
OPPOSITION	You may have a tendency to become too extravagant, and over spend. The money spent will probably be on gifts to yourself or for the ones you love. You will have a tendency to be overly emotional and won't be able to say "No" to any one wanting a favor. There may be a tendency to depend too much on luck. You should stay away from any get rich schemes. You may become very hypercritical of those around you and this may cause you trouble with them.

MOON TO SATURN

CONJUNCT	This aspect could cause you to become very serious, moody and depressed. You may find that your domestic affairs and relationship with mother, wife and females are very disturbing. The fickle public may appear to have turned their back on you. You may go through a very difficult emotional period now.

SEXTILE	This is an excellent time to help those less fortunate than yourself. This is a good time to make practical plans to be carried out at a future date.
SQUARE	This can be a very emotional and depressing period for you. You are probably very moody, suspicious and lethargic. Seems like you're exhausted all the time. Many upsets in the home; the home may need repairs that will cost you more than you can afford. You may be very anxious about work or your profession or business. Your income may not be meeting all the expenses at this time.
TRINE	This can be a very productive period. You are capable of intense concentration and prolonged physical activities. You are very serious at this time. You will and can accept more responsibilities. Your health will be improved under this aspect. More serious and mature women will be attracted to you.
OPPOSITION	This is a bad time to start any new investment program. This is also a bad aspect to invest in real estate because any property bought now will cost too much to remodel to make a profit. You may have disagreements with older people, the boss or your father. This could cause you to become very depressed because everything seems to come to a stand still. Wait until later to start anything.

MOON TO URANUS

CONJUNCT	Your ambitions and goals may be very unrealistic at this time. There are so many unexpected changes going on in your domestic life that it could cause you emotional upsets. You may be very tense and nervous which could cause health problems. You may have many muscle spasms. You can become very strong willed and stubborn over the smallest request.
SEXTILE	Your creative original thoughts and ideas will be accepted by others. Those in public life or in authority positions are receptive to you now. You may receive an unexpected promotion. You can think very rapidly and make instant decisions without any problems. Your thinking or mental processes are much keener during this period.
SQUARE	You may have trouble concentrating on any one thing until you have reached a satisfactory conclusion. You may have a tendency to be too strong willed and stubborn at this time. Your behavior may become very erratic and unpredictable so people will reject you. You are determined to do everything your own way or not at all, causing many arguments and quarrels with the public or females. There could be unexpected financial losses during this time.

TRINE	This can be a very productive time for you. Your judgment and insight are fantastic. Unfortunately, this aspect only lasts for a few hours. An excellent time to present any creative ideas or plans to the public for good results. This is a good time to deal with the public or public officials or those in the position of authority.
OPPOSITON	There is a tendency for much tension and nervousness involved in this aspect. Nothing seems to go fast enough for you. Slow down and avoid accidents. There could be many quarrels or arguments with women, wife or mother. The domestic life seems to be in a constant turmoil.

MOON TO NEPTUNE

CONJUNCT	Your emotions may be upset because your imagination is very active. You could get carried away with yourself. Your judgment may be affected because of your emotional upsets. You may have many vivid dreams now. Your emotions are so intense that they could create a lot of confusion in your life.
SEXTILE	For a writer, this aspect is very good. You could become very interested in poetry, science fiction or fiction stories. A very creative period for artists or musicians. Good time to study any occult or metaphysical subjects.
SQUARE	You will have a poor memory at this time. Your concentration is very poor and you will have trouble making a decision. You are probably so guillible at this time that you will be any easy prey for the first con artist who comes along. Your emotions will impair judgment to the point that you will question your own sanity. Promises made to you by others will not be fulfilled. The home life at this time is very upsetting and hectic. Some may be inclined to use drugs or alcohol to get away from it all.
TRINE	This is an excellent time to put your creative and inspirational ideas into use. This will help friendships and love affairs. You are too idealistic at this time. An excellent time to study any occult subject.
OPPOSITION	Your emotions could cause you to resort to drugs or alcohol to escape the confused conditions of your life and domestic affairs. If you have to make a decision at this time, check everything three or four times before you decide. This could he a very creative time for musicians and artists.

MOON TO PLUTO

CONJUNCT
You may become very active in public meetings or affairs. Your feelings will be very intense at this time but others may not be aware of them. Your income or business could improve.

SEXTILE
Discussing old problems with a more mature female may help you to solve them. It is an excellent time to get rid of odl, useless things in your life. Your directness and abrupt way of speaking may be softened by this aspect.

SQUARE
This aspect could cause some very intense emotional shocks and the final parting with a woman in your life. Control of your temper may slip. The family or friends' plans may be the opposite of yours. There may be many upsets in the domestic life. You may receive a costly repair bill at this time.

TRINE
Any unexpected, dramatic and permanent changes in your life can be adjusted to without any special effort. You may have an enjoyable love affair or take a trip for pleasure. You may increase your income by dealing with the public or with women. Your emotions are more stable than with the previous aspect.

OPPOSITION
There may be a strong desire at this time to go into seclusion to get away from all the confusion within your life. You may feel an intense desire to be first in everything. This could cause many quarrels or disagreements with those around you. A public official may be opposing your plans. There is a possibility of a financial loss in business. Don't trust anything to luck under this aspect.

TRANSIT PLANETS
TO PARS FORTUNAE

TRANSIT PLANETS CONJUNCT PARS FORTUNAE

PLANET

SUN
You will be able to impress the people around you because of your optimistic and cheerful attitude.

MOON
This should be a more relaxed period for you. Put forth effort to improve your profession and business.

MERCURY
Your judgement, thinking and concentration are very good at this time. Take care of any overdue correspondence and carry out any new plans you may have in mind.

VENUS
Your romances, love affairs and social life are very good at this time. You are very optimistic and cheerful during this period.

MARS
You may be very tense and nervous. Don't jump to any conclusions about anything; get all the facts.

JUPITER
This is a good luck period for your finances and income. You may tend to be too generous. Be careful!

SATURN
You may be very serious and thoughtful during this period. Any extra effort put forth at work will bring rewards at a later date.

URANUS
You may find yourself becoming too critical of others. Any extra effort put forth at work will reap unexpected rewards. Don't depend on your own knowledge; seek advice from experts or an experienced person.

NEPTUNE
All of your creative abilities and talents are at their peak. You can use these talents to help yourself and others.

PLUTO
There may be unusual and unexpected upsets in your personal life. Listen to the advice of your reliable friends. If you apply a little extra effort to what you are doing, you will succeed.